COULD I VOTE FOR A
MORMON FOR **PRESIDENT?**

COULD I VOTE FOR A MORMON FOR PRESIDENT?

an election-year guide to Mitt Romney's religion

Ryan T. Cragun
and **Rick Phillips**

Strange Violin Editions
Washington D.C.

FIRST EDITION, JULY 2012
Copyright © 2012 by Ryan T. Cragun and Rick Phillips

Strange Violin Editions
4200 Cathedral Avenue, NW, #702
Washington, DC 20016
http://strangeviolineditions.com

All rights reserved. No part of this publication may be reproduced or transmitted in any form or by any means, electronic or mechanical, including photocopy, recording, or any information storage and retrieval system, without permission in writing from the publisher, except for the inclusion of brief quotes in a review.

ISBN 978-0-9837484-5-8
ISBN 978-0-9837484-6-5 (e-book)

Library of Congress Control Number: 2012937944

Printed in the United States of America

TABLE OF CONTENTS

Acknowledgments ix

Introduction 1

Part I: The Basics 7

CHAPTER ONE 9
Is Mormonism a cult?

CHAPTER TWO 15
Okay, then is Mormonism a Christian religion?

CHAPTER THREE 23
Where did Mormons come from, and how did they get this way?

Part II: Practices 31

CHAPTER FOUR 33
What's the deal with polygamy?

CHAPTER FIVE 40
What happens inside Mormon temples?

CHAPTER SIX 50

Do Mormons really wear funny underwear?

CHAPTER SEVEN 55

Why can't Mormons drink coffee or tea?

CHAPTER EIGHT 59

What's up with all the missionaries?

Part III: Theology 69

CHAPTER NINE 71

Do Mormons really believe God lives near a giant star named Kolob?

CHAPTER TEN 75

Do Mormons believe men can become Gods? (And that God was once a man?)

CHAPTER ELEVEN 80

Do Mormons believe Jesus and Satan are brothers?

CHAPTER TWELVE 84

Who goes to Mormon heaven?

CHAPTER THIRTEEN 89

Do Mormons believe in the Bible?

Part IV: Social Issues 95

CHAPTER FOURTEEN 97

What do Mormons think about feminism?

CHAPTER FIFTEEN 102

What do Mormons think about abortion?

CHAPTER SIXTEEN 105

What do Mormons think about homosexuality?

CHAPTER SEVENTEEN 110

Are Mormons racist?

Part V: Looking Ahead 121

CHAPTER EIGHTEEN 123

Would a Mormon president take orders from Salt Lake City?

Conclusion 129

ACKNOWLEDGMENTS

Our families deserve a great deal of credit for making this book possible. Debi, Toren, Jany, Jonathan, and Sofia were all neglected more than they should have been so we could get this out in a hurry. Thank you, and sorry!

We also owe some credit to our extended families, particularly our parents, who raised us Mormon. While this may not be the type of book you dreamed we would write when we were growing up, do know that we love you and have written this book with you in mind.

We'd also like to thank our publisher, Strange Violin Editions, and editor, Therese Doucet, for seeing the merit in this project and taking it on knowing there was a lot to do in a very short time frame.

Finally, we'd like to thank Mitt Romney for running for president. We aren't voting for you in the general election, but we're glad you won the Republican primary. If you hadn't, this book would have been a bust!

INTRODUCTION

Mitt Romney has been hounded by questions about his membership in the Church of Jesus Christ of Latter-day Saints (otherwise known as the Mormon or LDS church) since he entered the national spotlight. Pundits and commentators across the political spectrum continue to argue over whether his arduous slog through the Republican nomination process was made even tougher because many Americans have misgivings about his religion. According to Gallup, about one in five Americans say they are unwilling to vote for a Mormon. Some of these people are Republicans, and others are Democrats and independents. Hesitant Republicans tend to cite theological issues as their main stumbling block. They're concerned that Mormons are not Christians, and they don't want to put a heretic in the White House. Democrats and independents tend to worry about where a Mormon might stand on social issues like abortion and gay rights. Some on both sides worry that if Mitt Romney is elected, the Mormon prophet in Salt Lake City will be calling the shots. Others are reluctant to vote for anyone who believes the weird things Mormons say they believe. Polls show Americans generally have negative views toward Mormons. Among religious groups, only atheists and Muslims are less popular.

This book is designed to demystify Mitt Romney's religion and address the major concerns – raised by both liberals and conservatives – about Mormonism. We aim to make the weird familiar. And you won't find many people more familiar with purported Mormon weirdness than us. Both of us are sociologists with PhDs who specialize in the study of Mormonism. Both of us have written extensively in scholarly journals on Mormon issues. Both of us are former presidents of the Mormon Social Science Association, a professional society comprised of scholars who study the church.

Aside from our academic credentials, we have an insider's perspective. We were raised Mormons in Utah. In fact, we grew up fifteen miles from each other, but didn't meet until our paths crossed at a meeting for sociologists of religion almost a decade ago. We are descended from the early pioneers who founded Mormon settlements in Utah. Our extended families on both sides consist of active members of the church. Both of us served full-time Mormon missions just like Mitt Romney, donning white shirts and ties and riding our bikes through town and country searching for potential converts. Ryan's mission was in Costa Rica, and Rick's was in Louisiana and along the Mississippi Gulf Coast. Both of us married Mormon women in a Mormon temple and participated in the sacred rites and rituals reserved for those in good standing with the faith. Ours was an archetypal Mormon upbringing. We were marinated in Mormonism from birth. That's why we're pretty confident that we know more than most pundits and commentators about Mitt Romney's religion, and how it might affect the way he would govern as Commander in Chief.

Now, we know what some of you are thinking: "If these guys are Mormons, how can I trust that what they say about Mormonism is unbiased and objective?" That's a good question. Here's our answer.

While we were once completely devout, these days both of us are estranged from the religion of our youth. Ryan severed all ties with the church when he was in graduate school and no longer considers himself a Mormon. Rick's situation is more complicated, but most church-going Mormons would consider him an apostate, even if he doesn't apply that label to himself. Our years of study and research led us (independently of one another) to conclude that the truth claims of the Church of Jesus Christ of Latter-day Saints are no more plausible than those of any other church. We don't believe that the visions and miracles attributed to Joseph Smith happened the way they were described to us in Sunday school. We don't believe that the Book of Mormon narrates actual, historical events, and we don't think it is any more inspired than the Bible, the Koran, or the Bhagavad Gita.

We're not beholden to the church in any way. We're not afraid that we'll get in trouble with ecclesiastical leaders if what we write deviates from the party line, and we don't think anything we say has an impact on our station in any afterlife. We're guided by the facts, and we're going to call it as we see it.

Of course, just as we've assuaged the concerns of those who might worry that our Mormon upbringing could compromise our objectivity, we've now upset those who think our disaffection from the faith will make us hostile or reflexively critical of the church. Is this book going to be some sort of anti-Mormon screed? No, that's not the case either.

Since we study Mormonism for a living, we constantly rub shoulders with first-rate Mormon scholars who know just as much as or more than we do about the church, but who nevertheless believe and practice their religion with the dedication and enthusiasm we had for the faith when we were young. We admit we haven't the foggiest clue how they pull this off, but we respect that they do, and we don't think they're deluded or disingenuous. Moreover, we love our Mormon relatives, and we recognize the important role the church plays in their lives. Being anti-Mormons would make us anti- some of the people we care about most in this world.

Besides, our commitment to calling it as we see it means not only dissenting from the church's party line when the facts dictate, but also defending the church when it is unfairly maligned – and that happens a lot. One of the things that prompted us to write this book was the egregious distortions of Mormon theology we've seen splashed all over the news. Reporters, politicians, and other public figures who should know better have been guilty of grossly mischaracterizing the beliefs of our family, friends, neighbors, and colleagues. We're happy to set the record straight when that's what the facts require.

Now, we're fully aware that one person's objectivity is someone else's bias. This is particularly true when you're trying to be "objective" about another person's religion. We're not naïve enough to think we can disabuse some Mormons of the idea that we're out to get the church. Mormons are particularly sensitive to attacks on their faith, and vitriolic critics of the church abound. A short session with an internet search engine and some Mormon-themed keywords can attest to that. But for some members of the church we know, any book that departs from the portrayal of the church in official LDS media outlets would be an anti-Mormon book.

That's why the "insider" perspective has its limitations. Lots of Mormons will tell you that if you want to know something about the church you should ask one of its members. But believing, devout Mormons have a bias as well. Since Latter-day Saints believe Mormonism is the true religion and the church hierarchy is directed by God, they are often unwilling or unable to acknowledge problems in church history or see the simple human errors of their leaders. For instance, in a subsequent chapter, we'll see how members of the church engage in mental gymnastics and employ pretzel logic to justify their founding prophet Joseph Smith's polygamy. After all, it's not easy to exonerate a man who claims God commanded him to sleep with his associates' wives and daughters in order to benefit them in the hereafter. Because we view Mormon leaders as mere mortals, we don't have to grope for ways to get the prophet off the hook. We think Mormon polygamy began as the institutionalization of Joseph Smith's philandering – a simple explanation that fits the facts and coincides with what psychologists say about the personalities of charismatic religious leaders.

In addition to their penchant for giving the church every benefit of every doubt, many Mormons are not particularly knowledgeable about their faith. Of course, this is true of any church. We teach courses on religion to university students who often profess their unshakable belief that the Bible is God's inerrant word. Yet we find that these same students often know very little about the Bible, and only a very few have read it cover to cover. That doesn't mean their beliefs are invalid, it just means when it comes to technical questions about the text of the Bible, you'd be better off asking a secular scholar who studies the book for a living rather than one of our devout students.

One way to think about the difference between the "insider" and "outsider" perspective when it comes to religion is to imagine a beautiful stained glass window. Seen from inside a cathedral, the window depicts a glowing, faith-promoting scene. Seen from the outside, the glow is gone, but you can see how the framework and panes of glass fit together to produce the image – not as pretty, but perhaps more informative. In some ways, we'd like to think we can relate to both these perspectives. We remember what it was like to be inside the church, but we're also scholars who make our living studying Mormonism with the tools of social science.

We hope we've convinced you that our approach to examining Mitt Romney's religion is a useful one. Even so, we don't expect you to accept what we say uncritically. At the end of each chapter we've compiled a list of recommended readings for those interested in further research. You can use these sources to continue your study or to check our facts and interpretations.

Finally, it's important we say one more thing in the interest of full disclosure. Neither one of us is voting for Mitt Romney. We're not interested in the message the Republicans are pushing this election cycle. Our views on economic and social issues differ fundamentally from Mitt Romney's, and frankly, we hope he loses. That said, our political predilections have *absolutely nothing* to do with Mitt's religion. We're writing this book to dispel some of the nonsense we hear about Mormonism as a result of his campaign. We want voters to make an informed decision about the issues when they cast their ballot this November, and providing the kind of accurate information we find sorely lacking in the news media is what this book is all about.

Part 1: The Basics

Is Mormonism a cult?

Okay, then is Mormonism a Christian religion?

Where did Mormons come from, and how did they get this way?

CHAPTER ONE

Is Mormonism a cult?

the soundbite

One person's cult is another person's denomination. Evangelical Christian pastors have long characterized Mormonism as a heretical cult, probably because Mormon missionaries are so good at stealing their sheep. But sociologists of religion (like us!) and other experts in the field don't see Mormonism this way. The beliefs and practices that guide Mormons in their everyday lives are surprisingly similar to those of Catholics and Evangelicals, and characterizing Mormons as cultists is silly and ignorant.

the details

Every so often, Mitt Romney dons a funny-looking ceremonial costume and engages in secret, arcane rituals that would appear bizarre (or ludicrous) to the average American. These rituals are hidden from public view in special Mormon temples set aside for this specific purpose. No one can enter these temples unless they are screened and approved by Mormon ecclesiastical leaders – and the entrance requirements are strict: you must give ten percent of your earnings to the church, drink no alcohol, coffee, or tea, and the list goes on. If this sounds more like the house party from *Eyes Wide Shut* than the services at your church or synagogue, then you may have some insight into why some people call Mormonism a cult.

Robert Jeffress, pastor of the gargantuan First Baptist Church of Dallas, made headlines on the campaign trail by declaring that Mitt Romney was not a Christian and Mitt's religion was a cult. A few months later, Franklin Graham, son of pastor laureate Billy Graham, made essentially the same claim on a prominent cable news show. These are just two of many such incidents, and rank-and-file Mormons in the United States are sadly accustomed to people calling their church a cult. But is this fair? Is it accurate? And what *is* a cult, anyway?

The word "cult" comes from Latin *cultus*, which means cultivation, care, or worship. When it first made its way into English by way of French in the seventeenth century, "cult" was synonymous with "religion." Over time, two distinct definitions of the word evolved. The first definition is what we'll call the sociological definition. Sociologists started using the word cult in the 1930s. They used it to describe new religious movements that were not obvious schisms of existing denominations, had novel beliefs, and were typically associated with a charismatic leader. For sociologists, the word cult is not meant to be pejorative, but rather descriptive. A cult is a type of religion, and sociologists contrast cults with "sects," "denominations," and other kinds of religious movements in this typology. This definition was widely used by specialists until the 1980s, when social scientists studying cults realized the term was acquiring negative connotations outside academia. These days, sociologists have dropped the term, and erstwhile cults have been dubbed "New Religious Movements," or NRMs for short. This label is free from the baggage that "cult" now carries. That baggage is the hallmark of the second definition of the word cult.

The second definition, widely used in popular culture, refers to religions that engage in weird or disturbing practices like brainwashing and mind control. Cults are secretive and mysterious. They isolate their members. They have strange modes of dress or engage in deviant sex. Some of them are dangerous, and people who get mixed up with them can wind up dead. You can thank what sociologists call the Anti-Cult Movement, or ACM, for this definition of the word. The ACM is comprised of people and groups that work to oppose new religious movements they deem harmful or dangerous. Human rights coalitions, "deprogrammers," former members, awareness groups, and research organizations are all part of the ACM. Sociologists who study the ACM point out that not every new religious movement has come under fire from activists. The ACM distinguishes between "destructive cults" and "benign cults," and they focus their firepower on the former. This does not suggest that benign cults are necessarily good, only that they are not as bad as destructive cults. (Kind of like benign tumors.)

In time, this popular definition of cult began to creep into the lexicon of certain conservative Christian pastors. They began using the term to describe religious denominations that espouse doctrines and practices outside the Christian mainstream, thus tarring these movements with the stigma of the Jonestown Massacre and the Moonies. Mormonism and the Jehovah's Witnesses are the two most commonly derided "Christian cults," and Evangelical pastors accuse the Mormons and Witnesses of following a counterfeit Jesus. They reason that Mormonism is dangerous and destructive because members of the LDS church cannot achieve salvation and are doomed to hell if they die while believing false doctrine. A quick internet search or visit to any Christian bookstore will reveal scores of web pages and pamphlets detailing the heresies of Mormonism.

Apart from doctrinal differences, some Evangelical pastors may have other reasons to be perturbed by the Mormons. The LDS church's ubiquitous missionaries are consummate proselytizers, and they work hard to convert anyone who will listen to their message. Hence, Mormons are a credible threat to these pastors' livelihood. Little wonder that some would choose to neutralize the threat by demonizing the Mormons. And what better way to do this than by putting them in league with Heaven's Gate and Scientology?

So is Mormonism a cult? Insightful readers can probably

guess what we're going to say. It depends on your definition. Consider the first, or sociological, definition. This is the notion that cults are new, distinctive, and heterodox, and often led by charismatic figures. Using these criteria, Mormonism began as a cult. Joseph Smith, the founder of the faith, was a self-proclaimed visionary and prophet. He assembled his followers together in dense enclaves where religion permeated all aspects of social life. His propensity for theological and social experimentation was so unnerving to their non-Mormon neighbors that he was eventually lynched. In a sociological sense, Mormonism in the 1840s was a classic cult, and Smith was a classic cult leader. But don't let your mind make the mistake of letting the connotations of our second definition taint this sociological definition. Remember, there's nothing pejorative about the word cult for sociologists. According to this definition, Christianity began as a cult that emerged from Judaism, and Jesus was the charismatic cult leader.

Nevertheless, just because a religion starts off as a cult doesn't mean it remains a cult. Most cults don't survive past the lives of the founding generation, and many fizzle when the charismatic founder dies or is otherwise deposed. But some persist, and these tend to survive by adapting and evolving. Adaptation and evolution usually move cults toward the social mainstream, and subsequent leaders of the movement tend to harness and routinize the charisma of the founder. Doctrines need to be codified, worship services need to have structure, and money has to be managed. All of this works to civilize religious movements that survive past the cult stage, morphing them over time into more conventional religious faiths. This civilizing process is clearly evident in the history of the Mormon church. As chapter 3 will show, the church has jettisoned many of the more radical doctrines introduced by its founder – like polygamy and economic communalism – in favor of an all-American image that eschews controversy and extols traditional Christian values. That's why we're comfortable calling 1840s Mormonism a cult, but we don't think the label applies now.

But what about definition number two? Robert Jeffress and Franklin Graham are prominent and highly visible Evangelical leaders. If they've pronounced Mormonism a cult, then there must be something to it, right? We don't think so – unless you're an ideologue cut from the same narrow-minded cloth as Jeffress and Graham. Evangelicals who label Mormonism a cult do so because they think the LDS church espouses doctrines incompatible with their interpretation of the Bible. But their interpretation of the Bible is pretty rigid and specific, and they don't allow much wiggle room. For folks like these, just about any church that falls outside their theological system is branded a cult. A quick internet search of the phrase "Is Roman Catholicism a Cult?" will reveal scores of websites hosted by Evangelical writers arguing in the affirmative. The arguments they advance are similar in form to those used to disparage Mormonism. We think labeling almost a quarter of the US population (and over a billion people worldwide) cultists is vacuous and stupid. Calling Mormons cultists is just as dumb.

We haven't minced words in our assessment of the Evangelical appropriation of the second definition of the word cult, but putting Jeffress and Graham aside, isn't Mormonism kind of weird in a cultish sort of way? Mormons may not practice brainwashing or mind control, and they may have abandoned their weird sexual practices over a hundred years ago . . . but didn't we start off this chapter with a vignette about Mitt Romney in a weird ceremonial costume practicing an esoteric, secret ritual hidden from public view? Sounds pretty culty, doesn't it? Actually, the truth is that we made it out to sound weirder than it is. You can learn all the gory details of what happens in Mormon temples by skipping ahead to chapter 5, but notwithstanding the admittedly unusual character of Mormon temple worship, most Latter-day Saints are normal, unassuming citizens with religious beliefs and attitudes that are remarkably compatible with those of their neighbors. The main reason why Evangelicals and Mormons tend to vote alike is because they think alike across a broad array of issues. That wouldn't be true if they were so radically different that Mormonism deserved to be labeled a cult.

suggestions for further reading

Any well-stocked Christian bookstore will have a "cult" section with books making the case that Mormonism is a heretical cult. Most of these are written by people who know surprisingly little about the LDS church. The most readable is probably Richard A. Abanes's *Becoming Gods: A Closer Look at 21st Century Mormonism* (Harvest House Publishers, 2004). For a scholarly view of the theological differences between Mormonism and Evangelical Christianity, see Donald W. Musser and David L. Paulsen, *Mormonism in Dialogue with Contemporary Christian Theologies* (Mercer University Press, 2007). For a believer's defense of Mormon theology against Evangelical critics like Robert Jeffress, see Ronald R. Zollinger, *Mere Mormonism* (CFI, 2010).

CHAPTER TWO

Okay, then is Mormonism a Christian religion?

the soundbite

So Mormonism isn't a cult. But is it a Christian religion? That depends on the criteria you use. Some Evangelical Protestants argue that because Mormonism does not accept the doctrine of the Trinity, the LDS church is promulgating a false doctrine of deity, and thus cannot be a Christian faith. Others argue that since the church espouses a belief in the divinity of Jesus Christ (albeit in a different way) and teaches that Jesus is the agent of salvation, it should be considered Christian. Most secular scholars who study Christianity accept this latter view.

the details

Most Mormons are pretty laid-back, but if you want to see the average Mormon freak out, accuse him or her of not being a Christian. Mormons find the charge that they are not Christians deeply offensive. In recent decades, emphasizing the church's Christian character has been the central component of the LDS church's public relations strategy. They point out that Jesus Christ is part of the church's official name, and in 1995 the church changed its logo to emphasize this fact, featuring Jesus's name in much larger type. LDS leaders also added the subtitle "Another Testament of Jesus Christ" to the Book of Mormon in 1982 to accentuate the book's Christ-centered theology. Mormons believe in the divinity of Jesus, they accept the virgin birth and literal resurrection of Jesus, and they teach that salvation can only be attained through the grace of Jesus Christ. Moreover, like most other Christians, Mormons are waiting for him to return. So what's the big deal? Why do some people claim that Mormonism isn't Christian?

Generally, those who say that Mormonism is not a Christian religion argue that the LDS church has a view of the Godhead that is not based on the Bible. The vast majority of Christians accept the view that the Godhead is comprised of a Holy Trinity. There are three distinct persons in the Trinity: the Father, the Son, and the Holy Spirit. Each of these persons is individually divine, but all three are one in substance. Thus, though there are three personages in the Trinity, there is only one God. Mormonism rejects this view, teaching instead that the Father, the Son, and the Holy Spirit are three separate beings. That means there are technically three Gods in the Mormon Godhead, and what makes them effectively "one" is their unity of purpose, not their unity of substance. Critics say this amounts to polytheism and contend that Mormons follow a different Jesus. They assert that the Mormon concept of God is simply not biblical.

The trouble is, many secular Bible scholars argue that the doctrine of the Trinity itself is not biblical and was a theological development of the second and third centuries designed to deal with a number of controversies that arose within early Christianity. Because Christianity emerged from Judaism, many early Christians were avowedly monotheistic. However, as the theology of the nascent Jesus movement developed, the divinity of Jesus became a vital doctrinal tenet. The Trinity allowed for strict monotheism and the divinity of Jesus to coexist.

Most scholars believe that our modern doctrine of the Trinity traces its roots to the Council of Nicaea in 325 CE – almost three hundred years after the death of Jesus, and almost two hundred years after the last book in the New Testament was written.

Readers will search in vain for any verse in the Bible that explicitly and unequivocally defines the Godhead in Trinitarian terms. The dearth of Biblical support for the Trinity led some scribes in the fifth century to insert a reference to the doctrine into the text of the First Epistle of John. The verse, known to New Testament scholars as the *Comma Johanneum* reads: "For there are three that bear record in heaven: The Father, the Word, and the Holy Ghost, and these three are one" (I John 5:7). This interpolation made it into the King James Version of the Bible in 1611, but later translations based on better manuscripts omit the verse or contain a footnote acknowledging that it is a later scribal addition. In sum, it is pretty easy to argue that the Evangelical concept of the Godhead is no more biblical than the Mormon view. As a Mormon missionary in the Bible belt, one of your authors (Phillips) recalls that it was pretty easy to argue Evangelicals to (at least) a draw on which version of the Godhead – Mormon or Trinitarian – was better grounded in scripture. The difference is, of course, that Mormon missionaries don't generally accuse those who disagree with them of not being Christians.

Just as in the previous chapter, where one's definition of "cult" determines how likely one is to apply the word to Mormonism, the definition of "Christian" one employs determines who is in the fold and who is a heretic. Since the Bible says a lot of different things about what qualifies someone as a true follower of Christ – which is the dictionary definition of Christian – different religious groups have come up with various ways of describing what constitutes a disciple. For instance, the Hutterites, a small sect that emerged from a reformation of Lutheranism in sixteenth-century Germany, believe that true Christians practice economic communalism and must be absolute pacifists. They base these beliefs on the Bible (see Acts 2:44 and 4:34). If the Hutterites are right, Evangelical Republicans are about as anti-Christian as it gets!

One can easily use the New Testament to make the case that Jesus asked his followers to give up all their material possessions, drop whatever they were doing, and dedicate their life to the gospel (see Luke 18:22, Matthew 6:25–34, and Matthew 4:18–20). If that's what it takes to be a follower of Christ – a "Christian," so to speak – then how many Christians do you know? We think you see the point we're trying to make. There is no accrediting body that serves as the official arbiter of which groups are rightly considered Christian and which are not. There is no objective standard – and we would argue no clear *biblical* standard – that enumerates the characteristics of a Christian church. Everybody's checklist is arbitrary. So when Evangelical leaders like Robert Jeffress and Franklin Graham claim that Mormonism is not Christian, just ask yourself: Who made them the boss? Where did they get the authority to determine who is or isn't a follower of Christ? Why is their contention that Mormons are not Christian any more authoritative than the assertion of millions of American Mormons that they are? Do you think they have the authority to make that call, or are they just dogmatists?

Litmus tests and membership requirements are the dogmatist's tools of the trade. The other day one of your authors saw a bumper sticker that read: "You can't be pro-choice and Catholic." This will come as a shock to millions of pro-choice Catholics around the country, and survey research shows that Catholic attitudes on abortion are not significantly different from the national average. (If you responded to this last sentence by saying, "Yeah, but they're not *real* Catholics," then you might be a dogmatist.)

Dogmatists come in many shapes and sizes, and dogmatism is not limited to religion. There is no shortage of people who will be happy to tell you what it takes to be a *true* environmentalist, a *real* Republican, a *genuine* wine aficionado, or an *authentic* fan of jazz music. But religion seems to provide very fertile soil for dogmatic thinking.

The Mormons themselves, who now complain and play the victim when their religion is maligned, have been very rigid and dogmatic in the past. Joseph Smith claimed that Jesus himself informed him – in person – that the religions of his day were "all wrong," that the various creeds of Christendom were "an abomination in his sight," and that ministers of the various faiths were "all corrupt." The Book of Mormon declares that there are really only two churches: the church of the Lamb of God, and the church of the devil. Unless you're a Mormon, guess where you belong! The Mormon temple ceremony used to depict a non-Mormon minister as a hireling of Satan, and nineteenth-century Mormon leaders often harshly denounced mainstream Christianity from the pulpit. John Taylor, a Mormon prophet, said non-Mormon Christianity was a "perfect pack of nonsense" and that "the devil could not invent a better engine to spread his work." Now that's not very ecumenical, is it? Modern Mormonism is much more restrained, but one could say what goes around has finally come around.

Mormons have attempted to distance themselves from mainstream Christianity in other ways as well. For instance, Mormons don't wear crosses, and their churches are not topped with crosses either. When asked why, members of the church are likely to respond that they worship the risen Christ and they don't want to fetishize his mode of execution. This is the answer we were taught in Sunday school as boys. But like so much of what we were taught in Sunday school, it doesn't tell the whole story. Throughout the nineteenth century, many Mormons wore crosses in the same way other Christians do today, but in the early twentieth century, church leaders began to discourage wearing crosses in a deliberate effort to distance the LDS church from other brands of Christianity. These days, if you see someone wearing a cross at a Mormon church service, you can bet that person is either a visitor or a new convert who hasn't been completely socialized into the Mormon way of doing things. Once again, the point is that in previous generations the LDS church had no desire to be lumped in with mainstream Christendom, and so it's kind of ironic that they are so adamant about being included today.

Since we're sociologists who study religion, we think it is useful to examine the way social scientists classify and categorize the various denominations that claim to be Christian. One classification scheme that was popular in the seventies and eighties separated the Catholics, Eastern and Oriental Orthodox Churches, and Protestantism into separate divisions. The latter was then subdivided into liberal, moderate, and conservative groups. From the outset, the terms "liberal," "moderate," and "conservative" referred to theological and not political orientations, although in recent decades the theological and political proclivities of Protestant denominations have become tightly consolidated. Episcopalians and Unitarian Universalists epitomize the liberal group, while the Southern Baptists and Pentecostals typify the conservatives. In this schema, Mormonism is considered a "Christian sect" and is lumped in with the Jehovah's Witnesses and Seventh Day Adventists. This is an acknowledgement that Mormons are well outside the Christian mainstream, but are still considered Christians.

Another popular typology differentiates between the Protestant "mainline" – venerable churches like the Presbyterians and the Methodists – and "evangelicals," who are newer, more literal in their views of scripture, and more oppositional in their approach to secular society. Here again, Mormons fall into an "other" category, but they are nevertheless defined as Christians.

Recently, however, these classification schemes have been losing their utility. American Christians are less and less likely to link their religious identity to a specific denomination. Increasingly, they are telling survey researchers they are "Christians" or "Born Again," instead of Baptists or Pentecostals. One of the fastest growing segments in American Christianity is the independent congregation with no denominational affiliation whatsoever. Independent congregations are, of course, stocked with independent members who don't belong to denominations either. As professors who teach the sociology of religion, we encounter scores of students who are devout, church-going Christians and have never been affiliated with a denomination. Even though their style of worship and theological views put them squarely in the conservative Protestant camp, if you ask them if they are Protestants they will likely say no or "What's a Protestant?"

Given this trend, what's to stop Mormons from identifying themselves as "Christians" to inquiring sociologists? Nothing! We simply don't know how many Latter-day Saints are now answering surveys that ask about their religion this way. Maybe none. Maybe lots.

Anyway, you get the gist. How religions and religious people choose to classify themselves is up to them. How academics choose to classify religions is up to them. And how religious bigots like Robert Jeffress choose to classify religions is up to them as well. There are no universally agreed upon criteria by which all people – academics, religious people, nonreligious people, etc. – can classify someone or some institution as Christian.

For the record, we've referred to Mormons as Christians in research presented at numerous academic conferences all across the country. We've called Mormons Christians in articles published in scholarly journals spanning the breadth of our careers. We have never encountered another scholar who raised even the slightest objection to this. It seems to us that for sociologists of religion – a bunch of non-dogmatists who know a lot about the subject – it's really not a matter of debate. Unless you've got a theological ax to grind, Mormons are Christians.

suggestions for further reading

Robert L. Millet, a BYU religion professor and one of the LDS church's leading intellectuals, defends the notion that Mormons are Christian in his book, *A Different Jesus?: The Christ of the Latter-day Saints* (Wm. B. Eerdmans, 2005). See also Stephen E. Robinson, *Are Mormons Christians?* (Bookcraft, 1991).

CHAPTER THREE

Where did Mormons come from, and how did they get this way?

the soundbite

Mormonism began with the religious experiences of Joseph Smith, the founder and first prophet of Mormonism. Smith attracted followers by claiming he regularly spoke directly to God and his new religion was the authentic restoration of primitive Christianity. The Mormons organized themselves into communities that experimented with theocracy and economic communalism. This did not endear them to their neighbors. After years of conflict, culminating in the assassination of Joseph Smith, the bulk of the Mormons traveled west to what is now Salt Lake City to practice their unusual faith in isolation. But their bizarre religious practices, epitomized by polygamy, kept them at odds with the government. Eventually, the Mormons were forced to abandon polygamy and assimilate into the American mainstream. Today, Mormons belong to an all-American faith and espouse values and political leanings very similar to other religious Americans.

the details

The Church of Jesus Christ of Latter-day Saints, also called the LDS or Mormon Church, is one of the nation's largest religious organizations. Members of the church call themselves Mormons, LDS, Latter-day Saints, or simply Saints. The Mormon Church has over six million members on its rolls in the United States, but scholars believe the number of people who identify as members of the faith is substantially smaller. Most Mormons live in the Western United States, and about a third live in Utah and southeastern Idaho. The church is headquartered in Salt Lake City, and Utah's population is about sixty percent Mormon. No other state is so dominated by one religious group, and the church wields considerable power and influence in Utah.

Mormonism had its origins in the religious experiences of a farm boy named Joseph Smith, who was born in 1805. In the 1820s, young Joseph lived in the Finger Lakes region of upstate New York. At the time, the region was suffused with religious enthusiasm, and itinerant preachers crisscrossed the countryside holding revivals and tent meetings to attract new followers. Official Mormon history tells us Joseph was confused by all this religious cacophony, observing that while the various preachers each claimed to speak for God, they disagreed and contradicted one another on fundamental issues. Joseph attempted to dispel his confusion by going directly to God for advice on which of the various churches he should join. In an account written almost two decades after the fact, Joseph claimed his prayer was answered by a vision of God the Father and Jesus Christ. In the vision he was instructed not to join any church, because they were all wrong. He later was told he would be the instrument through which God would establish the one true church – the Church of Jesus Christ of Latter-day Saints. (Earlier accounts of this experience, including the only one written by Joseph himself, are less detailed and less dramatic than the official account.)

A few years after this first vision, according to church-sanctioned accounts, an angel named Moroni visited Joseph. The angel told him about a sacred book written on gold plates. The book detailed the history and theology of the ancient inhabitants of the North American continent. Joseph acquired the plates, and under divine direction translated what was to become the Book of Mormon. His method of translation was a bit unorthodox. It involved putting a magic rock in a top hat, pressing his face around the brim to block out the light, and watching as the rock rendered the words on the plates into English. We're sure the engineers behind Google Translate would love to get their hands on this rock!

The Book of Mormon recounts the journey of a man named Lehi and his extended family, who fled Jerusalem just prior to the era of Jewish captivity by the Babylonians in 600 BCE. The family made its way to the sea, then traveled by boat to the Western Hemisphere. Once in the New World, Lehi's descendants multiplied and spread out across the virgin land. Some of Lehi's descendants were righteous and obedient to God. These were the Nephites. Others were sinful and rebellious. These were the Lamanites. Because of their sinful ways, God cursed the Lamanites and branded them with dark skin – something we'll discuss in detail in our chapter on race. The Book of Mormon describes the civilizations that emerged from these two tribes and contains prophetic writings, chronicles of warfare, and an account of a visit to the Americas by the resurrected Jesus. The book is named after a Nephite prophet named Mormon who compiled most of it, presumably by etching the narrative on the gold plates. Around 385 CE, the wicked Lamanites wiped out the Nephites in a genocidal war. Joseph Smith and other Mormon leaders taught that the various Native American tribes are the remnant of the barbarous Lamanites, though this view is not widely held among educated Mormons today. (Probably because it is demonstrably false.)

The sole surviving Nephite was Mormon's son Moroni – the same man who came back after death in the form of an angel to tell Joseph Smith about the gold plates. After the battle, Moroni added a few concluding thoughts to his father's anthology and purportedly buried the gold plates on a hillside in what is now western New York, where they remained hidden for fourteen hundred years before finally being delivered to Joseph for translation.

The publication of the Book of Mormon coincided with the organization of what would become the Church of Jesus Christ of Latter-day Saints. There were just six original members, but the church quickly took root and began to grow. Much of this growth is attributable to the hard work of dedicated missionaries. One of the most important and influential of these early missionaries was a man named Parley Pratt, whom some scholars have called the apostle Paul of Mormonism. Pratt, coincidentally, is the great-great grandfather of Mitt Romney.

Early Mormons believed that members of the church should live together in close proximity. The Mormons founded settlements in Ohio and Missouri, and all new converts were expected to gather to these locales. Steady streams of converts began arriving from Great Britain in the late 1830s, and Mormon communities swelled. However, the Mormons were not popular with their neighbors. Their clannishness and peculiar ways seemed threatening, and their habit of voting in a bloc gave them disproportionate political power. Many non-Mormons were also wary of the self-proclaimed prophet Joseph Smith, whose authority in the settlements was absolute. After a wildcat banking scandal ruined the church financially in Ohio, this settlement was abandoned. Subsequently, Missourians who were suspicious of the Mormons' abolitionism drove the Saints out of that state and across the Mississippi River into Western Illinois.

Once in Illinois, Joseph Smith's theological innovations became more frequent and more extreme. Most of the distinctive Mormon doctrines that set the church apart from the Christian mainstream trace their roots to the Illinois period. This includes Smith's most novel and controversial doctrine, the practice of polygamy. We discuss Mormon polygamy at length in chapter 4, but for now suffice it to say that the new doctrine did not go over well with many of Smith's followers, including his legal wife. Rumors of illicit sexual escapades involving Smith and his inner circle eventually made their way into a newspaper published by disgruntled former Mormons. In retaliation, the press that printed the paper was destroyed – an act that outraged non-Mormons in the region and eventually led to Smith's arrest. While Smith was in jail, vigilantes with painted faces stormed the building and gunned down the thirty-eight-year-old prophet.

The untimely death of Joseph Smith prompted a succession crisis within the church. Several splinter groups trace their provenance to this period. Some of these offshoots are still around today, though most are defunct. Eventually, the bulk of the Saints coalesced around the leadership of Brigham Young, one of the apostles of the church and an important confidant of Joseph Smith. Young believed the Mormons would never be allowed to practice their religion in peace within the United States, so he made plans to move the church outside the nation's borders to the Rocky Mountains, which was then Mexican territory. Young founded a new settlement in what is now Salt Lake City in 1847 and directed his followers to join him there. Thousands did. The story of the Mormons' trek across the plains by wagon and handcart is frequently cited as evidence of early church members' dedication to their religion in the face of hardship and persecution – even though most Mormons alive today do not have any ancestors who made the trip.

Young chose the valley of the Great Salt Lake as the new Mormon homeland because it was land no one else wanted. The valley was arid and had a short growing season. The Mormons were forced to depend on one another to eke out an existence, and the roots of their strong sense of community can be traced to these efforts. Once sequestered in the desert, the Mormons resumed their unusual religious practices without interference, including polygamy, which was announced publicly in 1853.

Mormon independence was short-lived. Under the Treaty of Guadalupe Hidalgo in 1848, Mexico ceded the valley of the Great Salt Lake and surrounding territory to the United States. Shortly thereafter, friction with the federal government began. Congress passed anti-polygamy laws specifically geared toward Mormonism. Mormon leaders were jailed, and economic sanctions were poised to bankrupt the church. Some polygamous Mormons fled to Canada and Mexico to avoid arrest, including Mitt Romney's immediate ancestors. Mitt's father George Romney was born in Colonia Dublán in Chihuahua, Mexico, which was an expatriate polygamist outpost. Eventually, the pressure Washington applied was too great, and the Mormons were forced to abandon polygamy and dismantle their theocratic government. The decision to dismantle polygamy led to more schisms, as many diehards refused to give up the practice. Some of the contemporary groups that garner media attention and infamy for their polygamous ways trace their roots to this time. These groups are often referred to as "fundamentalist Mormons" to distinguish them from "mainstream Mormons" who are now monogamous and headquartered in Salt Lake City.

Once polygamy was abandoned, Utah was quickly admitted to the Union, and the Mormons began to assimilate into the American mainstream. Starting in the early nineteen hundreds, the church began to downplay distinctive aspects of its theology and accentuated values it shared with the larger society, like the importance of family and patriotism. These efforts continue to this day, as we will note throughout this book. The church has worked to remake itself into a respectable and quintessentially American denomination. These changes have allowed it to expand outside Utah and to participate fully in the nation's economy. Nevertheless, Mormonism continues to be dogged by its peculiar past. The vestiges of nineteenth-century Mormon exoticism continue to compete with the increasingly idyllic – and mostly mythologized – image of the faith today. Nowhere is this conflict more readily observed than in Americans' reaction to the campaign of Mitt Romney, whose personal history is laced with Mormon peculiarity, but who is often criticized for being too perfect.

suggestions for further reading

An excellent, objective history of Mormonism is Matthew Bowman's *The Mormon People: The Making of an American Faith* (Random House, 2012). For a short history of Mormonism that can be read in one sitting, see Richard Lyman Bushman, *Mormonism: A Very Short Introduction* (Oxford University Press, 2008). Bushman is also the author of a scholarly, albeit sympathetic, biography of Joseph Smith entitled *Joseph Smith: Rough Stone Rolling* (Knopf, 2005). For a more critical appraisal of Smith, see Fawn M. Brodie's classic, *No Man Knows My History: The Life of Joseph Smith* (Knopf, 1945 – reprinted many times). For a history of Mormonism in the Utah era, see Thomas G. Alexander, *Mormonism in Transition: A History of the Latter-day Saints, 1890–1930* (University of Illinois Press, 1986). For a breezy, journalistic take on contemporary Mormonism, see Richard N. Ostling and Joan K. Ostling, *Mormon America: The Power and the Promise* (Harper One, 2007).

Part II: Practices

What's the deal with polygamy?

What happens inside Mormon temples?

Do Mormons really wear funny underwear?

Why can't Mormons drink coffee or tea?

What's up with all the missionaries?

CHAPTER FOUR

What's the Deal with Polygamy?

the soundbite

Mitt Romney only has one wife. If you heard one of the contenders for the Republican nomination had more than one wife, you're probably thinking of Newt Gingrich, who engaged in the non-marital equivalent of polygamy by cheating on his second wife with his third wife.

While not a polygamist himself, Mitt has polygamous roots. His great-grandfather, Helaman Pratt, was a polygamist who had at least four wives. Mitt is, no doubt, familiar with the fact that his great-grandfather was a polygamist, and familiar with the history of the Mormon Church and polygamy. But readers of this book may not be. Here's the skinny on Mormonism and polygamy.

the details

There's really no other way to say it: Joseph Smith was a horny guy. He cheated on Emma, his wife of nine years, with a teenage house servant named Fanny Alger sometime between 1833 and 1835. Fanny was only one of many sexual conquests. The best scholarly sources say that between 1833 and his death in 1844, Joseph married thirty-three additional wives, although estimates vary. Historians know that at least some (and perhaps most) of these marriages were consummated. Eleven of these women were currently married to other men when they became Joseph's wives. He married women in their fifties and girls as young as fourteen.

When it came to seduction, Joseph had a unique shtick. He apparently told his mistresses the Lord had commanded him to take other wives and they were now enjoined to help him do God's will. In the beginning, Joseph kept his practice of taking other wives a secret from Emma. But she eventually found out and was understandably livid. Joseph dealt with his domestic strife in a manner perfectly befitting an enterprising cad: he claimed to have received a revelation from God commanding Emma to accept the additional wives or be destroyed. Emma never really complied, and Joseph's polygamy is essentially what got him lynched in 1844.

The Mormons were a tight-knit group, and thus Joseph's dalliances were with other members of the church, including the daughters and wives of some of his closest associates. Ordinarily this would be a problem, but Joseph managed to use polygamy to solidify the loyalty of his inner circle by selectively inviting them to take plural wives for themselves.

While Mormon apologists typically claim polygamy was not about the sex, historians have noted that alternative sexual practices are common among the founders and leaders of communes and exotic religious movements. John Humphrey Noyes, a contemporary of Joseph Smith and founder of a commune called the Oneida Community, was dogged by sex crime charges. Noyes's community practiced a form of group marriage wherein young girls were initiated by older men and young boys were initiated by postmenopausal women. Jim Jones, the leader of the Peoples Temple, told both his male and female followers they were to be celibate and only he was allowed to have sex with them. And he did, with both the men and the women. Wayne Bent (a.k.a. Michael Travesser), who leads the Lord Our Righteousness Church, took the wives of his followers as his own and had ongoing sexual relations with his son's wife. The leaders of the offshoots and schisms of Mormonism that still practice polygamy are notorious for their licentiousness. Jeffrey Lundgren, the leader of a polygamous splinter group in the 1980s, took the wives of his male followers and claimed them as his own. The list of Mormon fundamentalists in jail for statutory rape or similar charges is long.

It seems religious leaders who charm their followers with charisma are often tempted to use the force of their personality to acquire things they desire, appropriately or otherwise. Just as politicians sometimes use the power of their office to seduce interns and staffers, religious leaders use the influence they have over their followers to gain sexual access to people who would otherwise be off-limits. Because so many people believed that Joseph Smith received regular messages from heaven, they accepted his instructions as if they came straight from God. It seems that among those loyal to him, only his wife – who probably had some insight into her husband's wandering eye – saw his extracurricular sexual activity as good old-fashioned philandering, divine revelations notwithstanding.

After Joseph's death, the inner circle kept polygamy as quiet as possible until the bulk of the church had arrived in Salt Lake City. Under the direction of Brigham Young, the practice was publicly unveiled in 1853. Brigham himself was a staunch proponent of what was called simply "the principle," and when it came to wives, he made Joseph Smith look like an amateur. Young had fifty-five wives, and the sprawling home he constructed to accommodate his enormous brood still stands in the heart of downtown Salt Lake. The novelist Orson Scott Card and NFL Hall of Fame quarterback Steve Young are both direct descendants of Brigham Young.

Once polygamy was out in the open, it was practiced by most of the Mormon hierarchy in Utah, and was common among local LDS leaders. It was not common among rank-and-file Mormon men, most of whom could barely afford to maintain one household. Taking a second wife was a mark of status in the community and a sign of loyalty to the church, since the Morrill

Anti-Bigamy Act, signed by Abraham Lincoln, prohibited polygamy in the United States territories.

Although it was technically illegal, the federal government could do little to enforce laws against polygamy while the Civil War raged. However, once the war ended, Washington turned its full attention to Brigham Young and company and began to tighten the screws. Mormons sought to challenge anti-polygamy statutes in the courts, arguing that such laws impinged on their First Amendment rights. Finally, in the 1878 case *Reynolds v. United States*, the Supreme Court ruled that claiming to follow a religious commandment could not be used as a defense in criminal court. Once the legal issues were out of the way, the pressure on the church became intolerable. Some polygamists – including Mitt Romney's family – fled to Mexico to avoid arrest. Others left for Canada.

In 1887, Congress passed the Edmunds-Tucker Act, which would essentially have dissolved the church and seized all its assets. This was the final straw for Wilford Woodruff, who became the new prophet the same year the law was passed. Woodruff waived the white flag and issued a "manifesto" stating that the church was no longer going to condone or perform polygamous marriages. While the 1890 Manifesto did not stop polygamy entirely, it signaled the beginning of the end. Clandestine plural marriages persisted, but such unions became increasingly risky, and by the first decade of the twentieth century they had all but died out. In 1904, president Joseph F. Smith, the namesake and nephew of the founding prophet, announced that the church would begin excommunicating anyone who entered into or presided over new polygamous marriages. Die-hards who refused to comply fled to the far reaches of the desert to found schismatic groups, but most members of the church were happy to see polygamy go.

The die-hards have come to be known as "Mormon fundamentalists." When applied to religious movements, the term "fundamentalism" connotes a strict, literal, uncompromising way of life and a combative relationship with mainstream society. Mormon fundamentalists are a contentious lot, and the communities they founded have always been vexed by leadership struggles. Some of these struggles have ended in violence, even murder. Fundamentalist communities are constantly splitting and fracturing, but they are in no danger of extinction. Scholars estimate there are between thirty and fifty thousand polygamists in the United States, and most of these live in the Intermountain West.

Most Mormons are aware of the church's polygamous past, and many find it objectionable. It's common to hear church members say they would not be involved in polygamy under any circumstances. They do not condone the lifestyle of Mormon fundamentalists or consider them compatriots. So how do they reconcile their personal disdain for polygamy with the behavior of early church leaders they revere as prophets? Some claim that a surplus of women in the church made polygamy a temporary necessity to ensure that every woman could have a husband. Unfortunately, this explanation doesn't fit the facts. Census data show that like most frontier areas, nineteenth-century Utah had a surplus of men.

Mormon apologists defend the character of Joseph Smith by arguing that he received his polygamy revelation almost a decade before he introduced the practice to his inner circle. Joseph apparently told confidants that he kept the revelation to himself and delayed publishing it for obvious reasons. But one day an angel with a drawn sword appeared and told him if he didn't unveil the doctrine he would be slain. This, of course, clears him of wrongdoing in the scandalous Fanny Alger affair. But we share his legal wife Emma's opinion that it was a little too convenient.

The LDS church hates it when the media refers to polygamous groups as Mormon fundamentalists. They desperately want to disassociate the words "Mormon" and "polygamy" in the public's mind. But scholars and journalists have used the term for decades, and they're probably not going to stop. This sometimes causes confusion. There are currently several groups who trace their religious lineage to Joseph Smith, revere the Book of Mormon, and practice polygamy. Members of these groups (and the organizations to which they belong) have a legitimate claim to the label "Mormon," but they are not members of Mitt Romney's church. These days any member of the Church of Jesus Christ of Latter-day Saints who takes a second wife will be summarily excommunicated, no ifs, ands, or buts. So don't be confused. The Mormon church has completely sworn off polygamy in this life.

But what about the next life?

One of Mormonism's distinctive doctrines is the belief that marriages solemnized in an LDS temple can remain intact beyond the grave. If you live a worthy life, the family you create on earth will remain with you forever. However, this opens up a "polygamy loophole" that allows men to have multiple wives in the hereafter under certain circumstances. If a Mormon man marries a woman in the temple and he suddenly finds himself a widower, he is free to marry again. If he marries a second woman in the temple and she is not currently "sealed" to another man, he'll have both wives in heaven. So even in modern Mormonism, polygamous marriages are routinely performed; it's just that these days the first wife has to be dead.

This is apparently the situation with a current Mormon apostle, Russell M. Nelson. When his first wife died, he married a woman who had never been married in an LDS temple. Nelson is, then, a future polygamist. However, he doesn't need to worry about being prosecuted for bigamy, since he won't live together with his wives until after he dies. Nelson's polygamous future is rather amusing in light of the fact that he has spoken out against gay marriage and claims that the ideal marriage is comprised of "one man and one woman." Mitt Romney – descended from polygamists – has said the same thing.

suggestions for further reading

An accessible and comprehensive introduction to Mormon polygamy is Richard Van Wagoner's *Mormon Polygamy: A History* (Signature Books, 1986). Also useful as a general introduction is Carmon Hardy's *Solemn Covenant: The Mormon Polygamous Passage* (University of Illinois Press, 1992). For an account of the sexual free-for-all in Joseph Smith's Nauvoo, see George D. Smith, *Nauvoo Polygamy: . . . But We Called it Celestial Marriage* (Signature Books, 2008). See also Todd Compton's award-winning *In Sacred Loneliness: The Plural Wives of Joseph Smith* (Signature Books, 1997). For a discussion of polygamy in early Utah, see Kathryn M. Daynes, *More Wives than One: Transformation of the Mormon Marriage System, 1840–1910* (University of Illinois Press, 2001). A good introduction to Mormon fundamentalism is Cardell K. Jacobson and Lara Burton, *Modern Polygamy in the United States: Historical, Cultural, and Legal Issues* (Oxford University Press, 2011).

CHAPTER FIVE

What happens inside Mormon temples?

the soundbite

We began chapter 1 with a vignette depicting Mitt Romney in a strange ceremonial costume engaging in arcane rites hidden from public view in Mormon temples. Temples are special buildings that are constructed for the sole purpose of hosting these rituals, and no one can enter a temple unless he or she is screened and approved by Mormon ecclesiastical leaders. What goes on inside the temple is so secret and regarded as so sacred that talking about it is taboo in Mormon circles. If either of us were to quote from certain sections of the temple ceremony, or perform parts of the ritual at one of our family reunions in Utah, it would elicit outrage and disgust. It might even get us punched in the nose. In this chapter, we're going to outline carefully what happens in a Mormon temple in a way that will be acceptable to most Mormon readers, while still giving others a sense of what it's like to participate in Mormonism's most mysterious rites. But for those who are too impatient to read the whole chapter, here's our one-sentence analysis of the ceremony: It's more boring than it is weird.

the details

The first rule of the temple is you don't talk about the temple. Most young Mormons who aren't old enough to enter the temple have no clue what happens inside. We grew up surrounded by temples, but because the taboo against talking about the temple ceremony was so deeply ingrained, we had only vague ideas about what transpired behind those walls.

Young men typically enter the temple for the first time when they are preparing to leave for their proselytizing missions (see chapter 8). Young women often go for the first time when they are about to get married. If you ask typical Mormons to recount how they felt after their initial visit to the temple, many will respond that it was an eye-opener. Mormon temple worship is very different from ordinary Sunday services, and some find the experience unsettling. However, despite the initial shock, most Mormons acclimate to the ceremony fairly quickly.

Before we write about the temple ceremony, it is important to give a little more information about the functions of Mormon temples. When Mormons refer to "the temple ceremony," they are really talking about a specific ceremony called "the endowment" – that's the weird, esoteric aspect of temple worship that Mormons won't talk about. However, the temple hosts other rituals that are linked to the endowment. The most common of these are baptism for the dead and weddings, which we'll now discuss in turn.

To the extent that non-Mormons have heard anything about the temple, they are most likely to have heard about the controversial Mormon practice of "baptism for the dead." Baptism for the dead does not refer to baptizing corpses, as the name implies, but rather to proxy baptism, meaning a living person is baptized on behalf of someone who is dead. In the Gospel of John, Jesus states, "Except a man be born of water and of the Spirit, he cannot enter into the kingdom of God." Thus, according to Mormon theology, there is no true salvation without the sacrament of baptism. Moreover, since Mormons believe theirs is the only true church, no other baptism will do. Anyone who converts to Mormonism must be baptized by Mormon authority, whether or not the person has already been baptized in another context. But what about all those people who lived and died without ever hearing the Mormon gospel? They can't go to heaven without a proper baptism, but it's not their fault they didn't have a chance to hear the truth.

Mormon theology solves this problem by granting people who have died without hearing and considering the message of Mormonism an opportunity to accept baptism beyond the grave. Mormons believe once you die, you go to a temporary spirit world where everyone awaits Armageddon and the final judgment (for more details see chapter 12). Just as it does on earth, the church has missionaries in this spirit world attempting to convert the dead before it is too late. But since spirits can't be baptized, it is necessary for someone on earth to be baptized on their behalf. Since no one knows who will or won't accept baptism on the other side, Mormons will perform a proxy baptism for anyone who has not already been baptized a member of the church. This, by the way, is one reason why Mormons are obsessed with genealogy. Right now Mormons believe there are perhaps millions of people in the spirit world who have accepted the teachings of the church, and finding their names and performing a baptism for them is considered a theological imperative.

The roots of this teaching are found in Paul's first epistle to the Corinthians in the New Testament, where the apostle talks about people who have been "baptized for the dead." This verse poses difficult problems for exegetes, and no one really knows what Paul meant. But the verse stuck in Joseph Smith's mind, and he introduced the practice of proxy baptism to his followers in 1840.

Not surprisingly, surviving descendants are often not keen on the idea of their dead relatives being converted to Mormonism in the hereafter, and controversy has surrounded the practice since 1995, when it was uncovered that the church had been providing proxy baptisms for both the Nazis and their Holocaust victims. (One of your authors [Cragun] remembers being baptized for someone named "Adolph Hitler" when he was about fourteen.) This controversy has erupted from time to time since 1995, most recently in early 2012 when it was discovered that the ordinance had been performed for the famous holocaust survivor and Nazi-hunter Simon Weisenthal and – for apparently the ninth time – Anne Frank.

Baptism for the dead is the only temple ritual that is regularly open to youth. Any Mormon over the age of twelve who has had his or her worthiness screened by church authorities can participate. The rite is simple and straightforward. Participants enter a room with a large baptismal font. In some temples the font is mounted on statues of twelve oxen, representing the twelve tribes of Israel. A Mormon man (only men can preside over the ritual) with the requisite authority to perform the baptism will wade into the font, followed by the person who is to be baptized. Males are baptized on behalf of other males, and females on behalf of other females. The baptizer grasps the participant with the left hand, raises his right hand, and says, "(Living person's name), having been commissioned of Jesus Christ, I baptize you for and in behalf of (dead person's name), who is dead, in the name of the Father, and of the Son, and of the Holy Ghost. Amen." Then the participant gets dunked. Mormons baptize by full immersion. The dunking gets repeated over and over again, and a person can be baptized dozens of times over the course of a ten- to fifteen-minute session. It is an efficient ritual. We both participated as teenagers, and we felt privileged to provide an essential sacrament for people who had died without the gospel. Mormons sometimes recount folk tales about the dead person who received the baptism making a supernatural appearance in the temple to thank the one being dunked on his or her behalf. One of your authors (Phillips) always implemented a strict regimen of scripture reading, prayer, and fasting on the day before going to the temple in order to be worthy to see such an apparition. Alas, no such luck.

Baptisms for the dead are always performed in Mormon temples, but ordinary baptisms usually take place in run-of-the-mill Mormon meeting houses, most of which are equipped with a font. However, any body of water with enough volume to support complete immersion will do, and baptisms can be performed in a pool, a river, the ocean... pretty much anywhere.

Another ritual performed in Mormon temples is marriage. Mormons can get married civilly, but marriages enacted by civil authorities are dissolved when one partner dies. Only marriage solemnized in a temple can endure for "time and all eternity." Moreover, according to LDS theology, no person can achieve complete salvation without being married in the temple.

Temple weddings aren't like typical weddings. There is no processional set to the Bridal Chorus. The bride's father does not "give her away." There are no flower girls or bridesmaids or groomsmen. There are no custom-written vows allowed. Even an exchange of rings is optional. Doesn't sound like much of a wedding, does it? So what *does* happen?

Every temple has one or more "sealing rooms" designed for Mormon weddings. At the center of the room is an altar ringed by a padded kneeler. The bride and groom kneel down, clasp hands, and face each other across the altar. A male officiator conducts the ceremony, overseen by two male witnesses who sit on either side of him. Sometimes the couple knows the officiator, but in most cases he is a temple worker who performs such marriages as part of his duties. Things commence with a homily delivered by the officiator. This is usually a short speech filled with generic platitudes, since he is unlikely to know the couple. The officiator then repeats a statement that performs the actual marriage. At certain points during the ceremony, a response is required from the bride and groom. They are instructed to answer "yes" instead of the more customary "I do." When the ceremony concludes, the bride and groom are invited to exchange rings if they have them and can share a modest kiss across the altar. (No tongue.) And that's it. The wedding is over. Only the closest of friends and family are invited to the wedding. Everyone in attendance must be screened and approved by their ecclesiastical leaders and dressed in white from head to toe. Mormon couples usually have fairly typical receptions later with a larger guest list, but receptions are not connected in any essential way to what goes on in the temple and have no theological significance.

Temple weddings have become controversial recently, because they marginalize people who are not members of the church, as well as those who are members but can't pass a worthiness screening. Lots of things can make a Mormon unworthy to enter the temple. Falling behind on tithing, skipping church a little too often, or having a little coffee with breakfast will all do the trick. You can live a life of perfect moral purity by the standards of most Christian denominations and still be barred from the temple. In practical terms, this means if you are not LDS or you are deemed unworthy, you will not be able to attend a temple wedding – even if it is your son or daughter getting married. It is common to see the parents of the bride or groom waiting outside the temple while their child is getting married inside. These parents will have to wait to offer hugs and congratulations until the new couple exits the building.

Mitt Romney had to deal with this issue. Mitt's father-in-law, Edward Davies, was an atheist and never joined the Mormon Church (though his children did baptize him by proxy after he died). He was unable to attend Mitt and Ann's temple wedding. However, in their case this concern was addressed by having a civil wedding at the Davies' home and then having the temple ordinance performed the next day. It sounds like a good compromise, but that solution won't work for American Mormons today. These days, couples in the United States who are married by civil authority must wait a year to have their marriage solemnized in the temple. This policy is designed to keep a civil wedding – with all its ostentation and extravagance – from overshadowing the simple and sacred temple ceremony. And isn't excluding your mom from your wedding a small price to pay for something so special?

The last major ritual performed in Mormon temples is by far the strangest. It is called the Endowment. We are not going to get specific about the content of the endowment ceremony, because as we explained earlier, revealing these things is taboo; it would pain our LDS families and friends and probably make our moms cry. Nevertheless, a transcript of the ceremony is available online at certain websites critical of Mormonism, and anyone handy with a search engine can find it in a jiffy. (Wikipedia even has a page on the endowment that spills the beans on some of the most secret parts.) Reenactments of the ceremony are available on YouTube, and parts of the rite were dramatized for the final season of HBO's "Big Love." In short, you can read the entire text of the rite and see filmed representations of most of it if you have the urge.

What we can tell you is that the endowment is a series of rituals in which participants learn about the history of the universe from before the creation of the world to beyond the final judgment. The story of the creation is dramatized, and God, Adam and Eve, and Satan are the central figures in the production. The expulsion of Adam and Eve from the Garden of Eden is critical to the plot. After the couple is evicted, they are forced to make do in the "lone and dreary world." But God, who is merciful, reveals to them hidden teachings that will allow them to return to his presence. As the ceremony proceeds, Adam and Eve acquire esoteric knowledge in the form of passwords and secret handshakes that will permit them to pass through the various barriers that stand between themselves and God's kingdom. The dramatization pauses from time to time and participants are provided with this knowledge as well (i.e., taught the passwords and handshakes). The endowment ceremony concludes when everyone symbolically dies, provides the passwords and handshakes to the Mormon equivalent of Charon the Ferryman, and enters the "celestial room" – a room in the temple representing the exalted celestial Kingdom of God. Every temple has a celestial room, and each one is well-lit and furnished with elegant but conservative sofas and chairs. Almost everything is white. Participants in the ceremony are invited to linger in the celestial room to meditate and ponder what they've experienced. It's the only place where one can speak openly about the endowment.

One important consequence of the endowment ceremony is that once a person is endowed, he or she is commanded to wear Mormon temple garments – a kind of ritual underwear – for the rest of his or her life. No more thongs. No more tighty-whities. (We discuss Mormon underwear at length in chapter 6.) In addition to ritual underwear, the endowment ceremony involves other types of clothing as well, and the temple vestments are imbued with symbolism. As with baptism, no one can enjoy true salvation without receiving the endowment. And just like baptism, Mormons go through the ritual once for themselves and then for a dead person each time thereafter.

The rituals in the endowment are strikingly similar to those used in Freemasonry, and historians with no theological stake in the matter believe the temple ceremony was modeled on Masonic rites. Joseph Smith founded a Masonic lodge in Nauvoo, and many members of the early Mormon hierarchy were masons, including Brigham Young and Joseph's brother Hyrum.

The endowment has changed substantially since it was introduced. Some of these changes involved removing weird things that used to freak people out. For example, the endowment ceremony used to specify exactly what would happen to you if you revealed the secrets that were being shared with you in the temple. The graphic nature of these penalties was softened in the 1920s, and they were removed altogether in 1990.

However, the most dramatic change to the ceremony came when the bulk of the rite was moved to film and audio recording. Before this, live actors portrayed the various characters in the creation story, and those participating in the endowment ceremony would move from one room to another as the rite progressed. This is how the set was changed for the performance. Once it was moved to film, the ceremony required fewer officiators, less space, and less time. This allowed more endowments to be performed, which is presumably a boon for the dead people waiting for them. Efficiency and volume always trump mystery and enigma with respect to the way contemporary Mormon rituals evolve.

This brings us to our last point about the endowment. Despite occasional rumors of orgies and devil worship in the temple that emerge from time to time, the truth is that the endowment ceremony is pretty low-key. Indeed, most of the stuff that is typically labeled weird is largely vestigial of nineteenth-century Mormon temple worship, which was a lot stranger than the modern version. Secret passwords and handshakes sound weird to the average citizen, but that's because these things are not associated with their brand of worship. As a matter of fact, if we had to pick one adjective to describe the endowment, we'd be tempted to say "boring." The film that accompanies the endowment is maddeningly dull and repetitive. People routinely fall asleep during the ceremony – including both of your authors in the past, regularly. We certainly wouldn't have dozed off during an orgy or a scary Satanic ritual, which is how Evangelical critics like to describe the endowment.

From our perspective, the endowment is not inherently weirder than, say, Catholic Mass, wherein a man in odd ceremonial garb turns a wafer into the body of Jesus and then leads the congregation in an act of ritual cannibalism. See how strange that can sound? One of your authors (Phillips) remembers being horrified by the cultic chants and strange synchronous movements of the celebrants the first time he visited a Mass as a teenager.

Still, if the thought of your president engaging in a ritual like the endowment makes you uneasy, recall that the temple ceremony is a close adaptation of Masonic rites. Fourteen US presidents (George Washington, James Monroe, Andrew Jackson, James Polk, James Buchanan, Andrew Johnson, James Garfield, William McKinley, Theodore Roosevelt, Howard Taft, Warren Harding, Franklin Roosevelt, Harry Truman, and Gerald Ford) were Freemasons, and presumably participated in rituals with crazy outfits and secret handshakes just like Mitt.

In sum, these are the kinds of things Mitt and Ann Romney would be doing if they went to the temple. Of course, we don't actually think they'll attend regularly if they're living in the White House. Mitt's huge security detail might compromise the sanctity of the temple, and given what we've described, it might be a public relations nightmare. But if a grandchild or close relative gets married while he's in office, Mitt might have to see his ecclesiastical leader to get approval to go inside.

suggestions for further reading

For an excellent introduction to the role of temples in Mormon life, see David John Buerger, *Mysteries of Godliness: A History of Mormon Temple Worship* (Smith Research Associates, 1994). For over-the-top anti-Mormon accounts of Mormon temple worship, see Chuck Sackett, *What's Going On In There? The Verbatim Text of the Mormon Temple Rituals Annotated and Explained by a Former Temple Worker* (Ex-Mormons for Jesus, 1982). See also William J. Schnoebelen and James R. Spencer, *Mormonism's Temple of Doom* (Triple J Publishers, 1987).

CHAPTER SIX

Do Mormons really wear funny underwear?

the soundbite

If you look closely at Mitt Romney's chest when he's wearing a white shirt, you'll see what Mormons call the "celestial smile," or the "eternal smile." The smile is produced by the low, arcing neckline of the ritual underwear worn by members of the church who have gone through the temple endowment ceremony. Mormons call this underwear "temple garments" or just "garments." Most Mormons are experts at spotting the smile, but anyone can see it if they look closely. If you want to verify that Mitt Romney is wearing his garments, wait until he's wearing a white dress shirt and look for a low hanging loop that curves roughly six to eight inches under his neck. That "smile" is the hem of the temple undershirt. The media often refer to temple garments as "magic Mormon underwear." Critics say they have occult symbols sewn on them. Is this true? Do Mormons believe their underwear has supernatural powers? What's up with the funny underwear?

the details

Our students are dumbfounded when we tell them Mormons wear special sacred underwear beneath their clothes at all times. They find it difficult to fathom that the omnipotent creator of the universe has a stake in anyone's choice of intimate apparel. But Mormons believe your underwear matters. In chapter 5 we wrote that donning the temple garments is part of the temple endowment ceremony. Mormon men usually start wearing them when they are around nineteen years old. Mormon women put them on when they get married, or if they remain unmarried into their mid-twenties they can go through the endowment ceremony and start wearing them. Once you put them on, you wear them for life. You can take them off for things like athletic activity and bathing, but aside from this, they must be worn continually. You have to sleep in them. You have to wear them when it's a hundred and five degrees in the shade. If you're a woman, you wear them under your bra. They may not peek out from underneath one's clothing, and they cannot be pinned back or rolled up to accommodate clothes that do not completely cover them.

Most temple garments these days are a two-piece ensemble, a top resembling a low-cut t-shirt and something akin to boxer shorts that extend to just above the knee. The female version has a lower neck, shorter sleeves, and is frillier. Styles and fabrics vary somewhat. A new version of the garment for men with a higher neckline is indistinguishable from normal white t-shirts. Mormons in the service can wear brown garments when they wear their uniform to conform to military standards. The temple garments are available in cotton, nylon mesh, and several different synthetic fabrics and blends.

The garment didn't always look this way. In the beginning, it was a jumpsuit that went from wrist to ankle. Early versions even had a collar. In the early twentieth century, the collar was scrapped and it was shortened to its current length. In 1979 a two-piece version made its debut. Many old people in the church had difficulty adjusting to the idea of two-piece garments and saw the change as an unacceptable accommodation to the wicked world. Nevertheless, the new garments were quickly adopted, and very few Mormons still opt for the jumpsuit.

Like the temple endowment ceremony described in chapter 5,

the temple garment was probably influenced by Freemasonry, and was introduced about the time that Joseph Smith was developing the temple ceremony. A number of symbols are stitched into the garment, and these have ritual significance. A V shape, called the "compass," is sewn over the left breast. The compass symbolizes the desire to live a life in accordance with God's commandments. A backward L, called "the square," is sewn over the right breast. The square signifies the exactness with which good Mormons strive to adhere to gospel principles. A dash, which has no official name, is sewn over the navel and serves to remind the wearer that the body and soul need constant nourishment. Finally, there is a mark just over the knee to acknowledge that every knee will soon bow in recognition that Jesus is the Savior of the world. These symbolic stitches are the source of the garment's holiness. When garments become worn out, the marks are to be cut out of the fabric and burned.

Wearing temple garments precludes adopting many contemporary fashions. This is the source of Mormons' reputation for modest dress. If you walk around Salt Lake City on a scorching summer day, you might be surprised by how few people are in shorts or tank tops. In places like Utah where Mormons predominate, wearing garments is an important marker of religious identity. Taking off the temple garment and reverting to regular underwear typically signifies the late stages of apostasy from Mormonism. We can assure you that right now in some bar in Salt Lake City, there are Mormons having a beer who would never dream of taking off their garments.

In the temple ceremony, the garments are imbued with the power to protect the wearer. Mormon lore is replete with urban legends about bullets bouncing off the garment or fire being repelled by the fabric. In a *60 Minutes* interview with Mike Wallace, J. Willard Marriott, a Mormon and hotel magnate who founded Marriott International, claimed that during a fiery boating accident, the parts of his body covered by the garments were not burned. Similar stories abound. Generally, however, Mormons don't take tales like these too seriously, and most believe that the garments are designed to protect the soul and not necessarily the body. For instance, it would be difficult for a devout Mormon to remove his or her garments to commit adultery knowing that an oath was sworn to remain faithful to one's spouse in the temple. Hence, one of the major functions of the temple garment is to remind Mormons of the promises they made to God during the endowment ceremony. So despite media reports to the contrary, Mormons do not think their underwear has magic powers.

But isn't it kind of weird?

We don't think so. From an anthropological perspective, many religions prescribe ritual or symbolic clothing for their members. The temple garment is much less obtrusive than the hijab, which is worn by millions of Muslim women all over the world. Orthodox Jews are a common sight in the nation's largest cities, and the skullcaps, or yarmulkes, they wear are also more visible than Mormon undergarments. Some Jews wear tzitzit and tallit. The tzitzit is a set of four tassels attached to a shawl – the tallit – that is worn under the shirt. The tassels are visible because they hang out from under the shirt. The tzizit is sometimes worn by little boys, and yet the same media commentators that make fun of Mormon underwear wouldn't dare mock Orthodox Jews.

So, yes, Mitt Romney wears "funny underwear," but religious clothing is pervasive around the world and worn unabashedly by millions of Muslims, Jews, Catholics, and others with little to no media commentary. So what if Mitt wears conservative, two-piece white underwear with symbols sewn into it? We'd rather picture him in that than a banana hammock.

suggestions for further reading

The best source of information about the development of the temple garment is David John Buerger's *The Mysteries of Godliness: A History of Mormon Temple Worship* (Signature Books, 2002).

CHAPTER SEVEN

Why can't Mormons drink coffee or tea?

the soundbite

If Mitt Romney is elected president of the United States, he won't be having tea with the Queen of England. There won't be friendly chats over beers in the Rose Garden to soothe hurt egos and resolve racial profiling conflicts. Because of his Mormon faith, Mitt Romney doesn't smoke tobacco or drink alcohol, coffee, or tea, and he doesn't use drugs that aren't prescribed by a physi-cian. While we're certain wine will still be served at White House social functions if he's elected, Mitt and Ann Romney will not be toasting with their guests. The Mormon dietary code, called the "word of wisdom" prohibits these things. So what's the big deal about a cup of coffee or a glass of wine?

the details

Mormons adhere to a dietary code called the "word of wisdom." You can read about it in section 89 of the Doctrine and Covenants, a book of Mormon scripture. As it is practiced today, the word of wisdom forbids the use of alcohol, tea, coffee, intoxicating drugs, and tobacco in all its forms. This is a rela-tively modest list of dietary dos and don'ts – Mormon rules for what you can and can't ingest are much less extensive and strict than the rules for Jews and Muslims.

Legend has it that when Mormon leaders met in Joseph Smith's house to discuss matters of church governance, they lit their pipes and chewed their tobacco. After the meetings, Joseph's wife Emma complained about having to smell the smoke and clean up errant globs of tobacco spit off the floor. After contemplating his wife's wrath, Joseph received the revelation that became the word of wisdom.

Aside from an admonition against tobacco, modern Mormon observance of the word of wisdom is not really based on Joseph's revelation, and many Mormons are surprised when they actually read the text of section 89. First, the word of wisdom is not presented as a commandment, but rather as sage advice from the mouth of the Almighty. The text says that wine should only be used for communion rituals and imbibing "strong drink" is not good. Mormons have always interpreted strong drink to mean alcohol in all of its forms. The revelation states that tobacco is "not for the body, neither for the belly." Similarly, hot drinks are "not for the body or belly." Today, this is interpreted as a general prohibition against coffee and tea. However, there are some inconsistencies with this interpretation. Iced coffee and iced tea are both against the word of wisdom, even though they are not hot drinks. Some Mormons claim that this is because they contain caffeine, and caffeinated beverages are prohibited under the "strong drink" rule. For this reason, some devout Mormons won't drink Coke, Pepsi, or Mountain Dew, because all of these sodas have caffeine in them. Curiously, however, there is no prohibition against hot chocolate, which is both hot and caffeinated. Finally, the word of wisdom suggests that meat is to be eaten sparingly and only in times of "winter, cold, or famine." This part of the revelation is completely ignored.

Some observers are befuddled by the fact that compliance with the word of wisdom in contemporary Mormonism bears no resemblance to the advice given in the revelation. But as sociologists we aren't surprised. We see the word of wisdom not as a dietary code, but rather as an important marker of religious identity and a way for Mormons to distinguish themselves from other Christians.

In the early years of the church, the word of wisdom was considered a guideline. Violations of the dietary code did not invoke any sanction. Observing the word of wisdom was not a prerequisite for entering the temple until 1921, and well into the twentieth century the use of tobacco was tolerated among older people who were set in their habits. Top leaders of the church were often inconsistent in their adherence to the revelation. Joseph Smith was known to drink beer. Brigham Young owned a saloon in Salt Lake City that served alcohol. But when Utah was admitted to the union in 1896 and polygamy was abandoned, church leaders began to emphasize the word of wisdom as a way to maintain the boundary between Mormons and the larger society. Many of the first non-LDS immigrants to Utah were hard drinking miners and railroad workers. By prohibiting alcohol and tobacco, the church inhibited social relationships between its members and those outside the faith. Christian Smith, a leading sociologist of religion, argues that religious groups often thrive as a result of beliefs and practices that separate them from society, because such practices increase solidarity within the group and highlight the boundary between the righteous and the profane. These days, the word of wisdom is an essential element of Mormon identity. The prohibition on alcohol is so complete that water is now used for communion instead of wine. Intoxicating drugs are also considered part of the revelation, even though they are not mentioned in the text at all.

As a guideline for healthy living, the word of wisdom is pretty good advice. Everyone knows tobacco is harmful and addictive. Intoxicating drugs can destroy lives and relationships. Excessive alcohol use is also dangerous and destructive, although moderate alcohol use has health benefits. Likewise, the health risks of coffee and tea may be offset by their benefits. The admonition to use meat sparingly makes medical, environmental, and economic sense, but many Mormons don't even know this is part of the word of wisdom.

Research shows that Mormons live longer, healthier lives than the average American. This may be due to their abstinence from things like cigarettes and beer. Some members of the church claim this health and longevity is evidence that Joseph Smith was a prophet, because his dietary advice was published before there was any peer-reviewed science to back him up. But many contemporaries of Joseph Smith advocated dietary restrictions that were nearly identical to the word of wisdom. There were proponents of vegetarianism who believed meat should be avoided whenever possible. The temperance societies that eventually succeeded in criminalizing the possession of alcohol in the United States were active in Joseph's day. People like Sylvester Graham, the inventor of Graham crackers, recommended similar diets before Joseph Smith did, using nearly identical language. Hence, rather than showing that he was ahead of his time, the word of wisdom demonstrates that Joseph was a product of his time.

We are pretty sure Mitt Romney keeps the word of wisdom. We know many Mormons in our Utah hometowns who are in their seventies and eighties and have never imbibed a single drop of alcohol or had a cup of coffee. The odds are good this describes Mitt as well. Thus far, Mitt's teetotalism hasn't really raised eyebrows. It's just not that odd to abstain from alcohol and tobacco in America these days. Besides, given the amount of stress that goes along with the presidency, if Mitt Romney ends up in the White House, it will probably be a good thing he doesn't drink.

suggestions for further reading

An exhaustive analysis of the word of wisdom is Paul H. Peterson's *An Historical Analysis of the Word of Wisdom* (Benchmark Books, 2005).

CHAPTER EIGHT

What's up with all the missionaries?

the soundbite

You've probably seen them riding their bikes or walking down the streets of your town. They're dressed in white shirts, ties, and dark pants and have prominent black name tags. They may have even knocked on your door. They are the ubiquitous Mormon missionaries. Last year there were around fifty-five thousand of them preaching the Mormon gospel on six continents, from the Arctic Circle to Tierra del Fuego, from Bogota to Bangkok. Mitt Romney served a Mormon mission in France from 1966 to 1968. He knocked on doors and passed out tracts attempting to get people to join the Mormon church. Why does the LDS church send out so many missionaries? Who goes on these missions? What is the life of a Mormon missionary like?

the details

Mormons have been involved in missionizing since the church was founded in 1830. Joseph Smith taught that his new gospel was the only true religion on the face of the earth, and thus the salvation of every living soul was at stake. Spreading the Mormon gospel was a vital concern from the outset. The first missionaries were not typically young, single men in their late teens and early twenties like they are today. They were middle-aged men, often with families, who traveled alone and relied on the kindness of strangers for room and board.

Sometime in the first half of the twentieth century, the composition of the church's missionary force changed. Instead of asking married men to interrupt their careers and leave their families to go on missions, the church began calling nineteen-year-old boys instead. Nineteen-year-olds are generally less encumbered by grown-up responsibilities that might make going on a mission an economic or domestic hardship, but they are still mature enough to learn the proselytizing techniques employed by the church. Today, young men make up the bulk of the missionary corps, but there are two other groups who can serve missions as well. Single young women are allowed to go when they reach the age of twenty-one. In Mormon circles, women are expected to be married or on the verge of marriage at twenty-one, so "sister missionaries" have traditionally been stigmatized as women no one wants to marry. These days, however, Mormons are waiting a little longer to get married, and this stigma is diminishing. Unlike the men, who serve for two years, sisters serve for just eighteen months. The other group that makes up the missionary force is retired couples, who use their savings to finance their service to the church.

Sisters and retired couples can serve if they want, but all young men who are physically and mentally able are expected to serve for two years. In Utah, where Mormonism is the majority faith, a great deal of social pressure is placed on young men who are reluctant to serve a mission. One of your authors (Phillips) had no desire to go, but went anyway, for fear that no good Mormon girl would ever date a boy who hadn't served a mission – a legitimate fear in Utah at the time. Nevertheless, despite these pressures, fewer and fewer young men are choosing to go. In the 1990s, close to sixty-five thousand Mormons were serving full-time missions. As we're writing this, there are about fifty-five thousand in the field, even though the church is much larger now.

The Mormon missionary system is a vast, bureaucratic enterprise. Young men who are interested in serving are asked to meet with their ecclesiastical leaders in the months before they turn nineteen and submit an application to go on a mission. If the paperwork is done and they are deemed morally, physically, and mentally fit, a mission assignment, or "call," is handed down from the church hierarchy in Salt Lake City. Missionaries are assigned to a location based on a variety of factors, including prior language experience, personal health, and the availability of visas.

Once a missionary is called to a mission, he (or she) reports to one of the church's Missionary Training Centers. As of 2012, there are seventeen such centers throughout the world. The largest and oldest is in Provo, Utah, adjacent to the campus of Brigham Young University. If a missionary does not need to learn a foreign language, then training lasts about three weeks. If the missionary does need to learn a language, then he (or she) is sent to the training center in Provo for twelve weeks of intensive language instruction.

Once training is complete, missionaries go to their assigned proselytizing mission. The mission is overseen by a mission president, typically a mature man who has lived a life of exemplary service to the church. Mission presidents are rarely engaged in proselytizing themselves, and spend their time managing and mentoring the missionaries. The leadership style of mission presidents varies. Rick recalls his mission president as an authoritarian taskmaster who motivated the young men he supervised with guilt and fear. Ryan's first mission president spent most of his time trying to rein in the misbehavior of the missionaries in Costa Rica. The previous mission president was lax when it came to enforcing rules, leading many missionaries to slack off and break mission rules (see below). He was kind-hearted, but strict enough occasionally to send a missionary home. Ryan's second mission president was from Colombia and was a convert to the Church. He was not particularly knowledgeable about Mormonism and knew next to nothing about proselytizing, but he was an able manager of people from years of running the family business.

Mormon missionaries are not allowed to use their first names. As we mentioned earlier, female missionaries are given the title "Sister," while male missionaries are called "Elders" – a title some find strange for nineteen-year-old boys. These titles are coupled with the missionaries' last names, as in "Elder Phillips" or "Sister Cragun." Missionaries are not to call one another by their first name.

Missionaries live and work in pairs, called "companionships." Unless they're in the bathroom, missionaries must be in the presence of their companion at all times. No running to the store on an errand by yourself. No going for a solo jog. On our missions, companionships that lived in two-bedroom apartments were required to share a room so that they would not be sleeping alone. The inseparability of companionships means that missionaries are always monitoring and modulating one another's behavior. This makes it difficult (but not impossible) to break the strict and extensive mission rules. In some missions, this gets taken to extremes. For example, Rick's mission president was constantly warning missionaries about the evils of masturbation and required that the bathroom door remain ajar during showers. This policy was designed to raise the stakes for any missionary who might contemplate a furtive wank at bath time.

Mormon missionaries are required to follow all of the behavioral restrictions other Mormons must follow – no tobacco or alcohol, no coffee or tea, no drugs, no swearing, no pre-marital sex, etc. But in addition to these behavioral restrictions, there are also heaps of additional rules. Add them all up, and it sounds pretty draconian. Missionaries can't listen to the radio. They can't watch TV or attend movies that haven't been pre-approved by their leaders. They aren't supposed to read the newspaper. They can't have a beard or mustache. Any contact with the opposite sex that might look remotely like courtship is forbidden. Also, and more curiously, missionaries are not allowed to swim. No one knows exactly why swimming is prohibited, but mission lore is replete with rumors that Satan has heightened powers in the water. It is more likely, however, that the prohibition is designed to keep missionaries from seeing girls in skimpy bathing suits. It may also be forbidden because swimming is risky, and comparable risky activities are also banned, such as skiing, rock climbing, riding a horse, and recreational boating or flying.

The missionaries' daily schedule is highly regimented. They must rise in the morning by 6:30 a.m., dress and eat breakfast, and spend time studying the scriptures, both individually and as a companionship. They are expected to be out the door and looking for converts by 9:30 a.m. They work until at least 9 p.m., with short breaks for lunch and dinner. Missionaries frequently eat at the homes of church members, where they often push their hosts to give them the names of friends and associates to track down. They follow this schedule six days a week, with one weekday off, called "preparation day," or "P-day." This day is set aside for laundry, grocery shopping, and wholesome recreation. P-day is also used for writing letters to friends and family. (Missionary letters sent by post are not censored, but emails are only allowed through an email system controlled by the church that is filtered and censored.) Preparation day begins after morning scripture study and ends after dinner. So even on their day off, missionaries don't get the evening off. When traveling on P-day they are still required to wear white shirts, name tags, and ties, but they can change out of their dress clothes to play sports.

If all of these rules and regulations sound oppressive and invasive, it's because they are – by design. Mormon missions are an example of what sociologists call a "total institution." A total institution is a social organization that is designed to cut its members off from society and impose rules and regimens that remake a person's identity. Missionaries can't call home to talk to friends, and they can only speak to their family on Christmas and Mother's Day. They refer to one another by title rather than by name. Their dark suits, white shirts, and conservative ties constitute a uniform that every missionary must wear, day in and day out. Their odd appearance and unusual behavior marks them for ridicule, which the missionaries interpret as evidence that the world is wicked and the forces of evil are intent on thwarting them. Isolation and depersonalization increases dependence on mission leaders, and being cut off from all media that isn't screened by the church keeps any ideas or thoughts that might compete with Mormon theology out of their heads.

It is not surprising that some missionaries have a long period adjusting to normal life when they return. We distinctly remember how weird it felt to be alone and free for the first time after two years of constant monitoring. While most Mormons report that they enjoyed their missions, it isn't hard to find returned missionaries who feel embittered and scarred by the experience.

Of course, despite all these methods to ensure obedience, some missionaries manage to break the rules. Most of them are, after all, nineteen-year-old boys. Missionaries get sent home from their missions – the Mormon equivalent of a dishonorable discharge – all the time for rule infractions. We've heard of missionaries getting the boot for having sex, getting drunk, smoking pot, looking at porn, scuba diving, getting married, gambling, and a variety of other sins. Sometimes one companion gets in trouble by himself. For example, missionaries have been known to sneak out of their apartment after their companion is asleep to meet up with girls. Occasionally companionships go rogue together. For instance, chance – or (mis)fortune, depending on how you look at it – sometimes puts two gay elders together, with predictable results.

For the most part, young men are not typically well versed in theology or religious literature, so the missionary training centers provide a crash course in Mormon doctrine and the techniques for teaching this doctrine to people who might be interested in joining the church. The missionary lessons have changed considerably over the past few decades, but the general message is the same: Joseph Smith was called by God to restore the true church to the earth, and the evidence of this restoration is embodied in the Book of Mormon.

Proselytizing methods vary. One way missionaries meet people is by striking up conversations with random strangers wherever they are encountered: on the street, on the bus, or in the store. As you might expect, this is not a very effective way to find converts. Missionaries also go through the neighborhoods in their area knocking on doors. This is known as "tracting," and it also has a low success rate, although people are sometimes converted this way. Another proselytizing method involves following up on referrals provided by members of the church. Mormons live by the motto "every member a missionary," and they often bring up their religion with friends and co-workers when they see an opening. If these associates are interested in learning more, their names are passed on to the missionaries for formal religious instruction. This is much more successful than the various forms of "cold calling," because contact with the missionaries is initiated by someone the person knows and trusts. Because such referrals improve the odds of conversion, mis-sionaries often push members of the church to provide them with names. Finally, missionaries visit with members of the church who no longer attend worship services in an effort to reactivate them. Some observers estimate that at least half of all Mormons on church rolls are completely inactive, so there are plenty of lapsed members to visit.

At this point you may be asking, "Who pays for all these missionaries living and working in every corner of the globe?" The answer is that the missionaries and their families pay most of the bills. Mormon parents often begin saving for their child's mission when he or she is very young, and many LDS children have a mission savings account or piggy bank where they put money from babysitting and mowing lawns. However, no worthy, capable young man or woman is turned away for being too poor to finance a mission. In cases where the family can't scrape together the funds, the church provides them. Most missionaries who come from poor countries are subsidized by the church.

When a family is providing money to finance a missionary, that money doesn't go from the family's bank account straight to the missionary's. Rather, a set sum goes to the church every month, and that money is pooled together, divided up, and disbursed to the missionaries in the field. Missionaries in more expensive countries – like Denmark or Japan – receive larger monthly stipends than missionaries in poor countries like Haiti or Nigeria. But the families of missionaries in all these countries send the same amount to Salt Lake City each month. We find it more than a little ironic that a church teeming with conservative Republicans finances its largest bureaucratic initiative via a centralized system of disbursement and the redistribution of wealth.

The mission experience is an important rite of passage for young Mormon men, particularly in Utah, where participation is expected. As little children, Mormons sing a song called, "I Hope They Call Me on a Mission," which extols the virtues of missionary work and emphasizes the centrality of proselytizing in the LDS church. Mormons believe that since these are the last days and the world is filled with sin, it is vital that everyone be given an opportunity to hear the gospel. It is possible that these kinds of theological concerns motivated young Willard Mitt Romney to pack his bags and depart for France in 1966.

Full-time missions last two years, but recall the adage "every member a missionary." If sharing the gospel is expected of every Mormon, then shouldn't we worry that Mitt Romney might use his position as president of the United States to try to convert people to Mormonism? Probably not. It's hard for us to imagine him handing out copies of the Book of Mormon at cabinet meetings or asking the Chairman of the Joint Chiefs of Staff if he'd like to sit down with the elders. No one ever accused Mitt Romney of proselytizing while he was governor of Massachusetts, and since the Bay State is consistently forty-ninth or fiftieth in per capita Mormons, the church could have used his help. It is more likely that if people are converted to Mormonism by Mitt Romney, it will be by following his example. If Mitt wins, it is possible that some people might be attracted to Mormonism because the president is LDS. Good Mormons live wholesome lives that are centered on family, and many people see this as a virtue to emulate. Many new converts say that they first started investigating the church because of the exemplary life of a Mormon neighbor.

However, it is equally likely that if Mitt is an unpopular president, the church might sustain some collateral damage. The church has received an enormous amount of bad press for its political activity and its early doctrines. Things like the *Book of Mormon* musical now playing on Broadway and a steady stream of jokes from late-night talk show hosts have cast a spotlight on the Mormons' dirty laundry. Things that had been swept under the rug for decades are now being uncovered, and it's hard to see when it will end. A lot of this can be attributed to Mitt Romney's run for the presidency, and perhaps that's why he has been quiet about his faith, and why we think he'll continue to keep quiet if he is elected.

Finally, evidence suggests that after a period of meteoric growth, interest in Mormonism – both within the United States and internationally – has cooled. Rates of conversion have slowed, and rates of defection from the church are rising. Part of the reason for this is that Americans are becoming more ecumenical. They are less and less likely to believe that there is only one true church or only one way to heaven. An exclusive claim to the big-T "Truth" is central to the Mormon message, and so the church's exclusionary theology is a product that fewer people are interested in buying. While any religion with a missionary program as huge as the one managed by the Mormons will bring in lots of converts, the number of converts per missionary has declined. Indeed, recent surveys show that a surprising number of Mormons themselves agree that there is not just one way to heaven and there is probably more than one "true" church. In short, sociological data suggest that the product the Mormon missionaries are selling is a bit dated. Nevertheless, we're sure they'll keep right on selling. But don't fret, Mitt Romney won't be part of the sales force.

suggestions for further reading

Not much scholarly work has been done on Mormon missions. One exception is a book by twin brothers Gary and Gordon Shepherd entitled *Mormon Passage: A Missionary Chronicle* (University of Illinois Press, 1998). The Shepherds used their extensive missionary journals to write an account of what their life was like as proselytizing elders. For a non-Mormon perspective on Mormon missionaries, Rob Lively Jr. provides useful insights in a 1993 article published in *BYU Studies*, "A Non-Mormon Religion Professor's Impressions of Mormon Missionaries" (volume 33, number 1).

Part III: Theology

Do Mormons really believe God lives near a giant star named Kolob?

Do Mormons believe men can become Gods? (And that God was once a man?)

Do Mormons believe Jesus and Satan are brothers?

Who goes to Mormon heaven?

Do Mormons believe in the Bible?

CHAPTER NINE

Do Mormons really believe God lives near a giant star named Kolob?

the soundbite

In the Tony Award–winning Broadway show *The Book of Mormon*, one of the central characters, the LDS missionary Elder Price, sings with conviction that he believes God lives on a planet called Kolob. The line draws a big laugh from the audience. After all, who could possibly believe something so bizarre? In fact, the idea that God lives near a star named Kolob is enshrined in Mormon scripture, and it's certainly something Mitt Romney was taught from a very early age. Hence, although they're loath to talk about it these days, Mormons really do believe God lives near a giant star named Kolob.

the details

Joseph Smith was obsessed with ancient texts and exotic languages. He claimed to have translated the Book of Mormon from a language he identified as "Reformed Egyptian" into English via divine revelation and the aid of a magic rock. In 1835, an antiquities dealer named Michael Chandler, who operated a travelling exhibit featuring Egyptian mummies and manuscripts, called on Joseph in the Mormon settlement of Kirtland, Ohio. Chandler had heard of the prophet's reputation as a translator of ancient documents, and he wanted to see if Joseph could read the hieroglyphics on some ancient Egyptian papyri. Captivated by Chandler's papyrus scrolls, Joseph arranged to purchase them.

Once they were in his possession, Joseph made the grandiose claim that the papyri contained the writings of the patriarch Abraham "by his own hand upon papyrus." Joseph set to work on an Egyptian alphabet and grammar and began producing a text interpreting the scenes on the scrolls. It turns out that modern Egyptologists have identified these papyri as common, ordinary funerary documents. Such documents were often entombed with mummies, and many examples comparable to the ones purchased by Joseph Smith are known to scholars of ancient Egypt. Nevertheless, Joseph's "translation" of the papyri became known as the Book of Abraham – an esoteric book of Mormon scripture that centers on the life of the patriarch Abraham and introduces some very strange ideas about cosmology and the nature of God. The Egyptian papyri provided a convenient way for Joseph to update the theology of his new religious movement with ideas he had developed since the publication of the Book of Mormon. In fact, the Joseph Smith papyri do not date to the time of Abraham, and the writing on the scrolls – which has since been translated by qualified Egyptologists – bears no resemblance whatsoever to Joseph's rendering. These facts have become very inconvenient for the church, and the Book of Abraham has become something of an embarrassment to many educated Mormons these days.

Observers have noted similarities between the content of the Book of Abraham and the writings of the philosopher and theologian Thomas Dick (1774–1857). Passages from Dick's work were published in a Mormon periodical right around the time Joseph "translated" the papyri, and many of the themes in the Book of Abraham seem derived from Dick's best known book, *Philosophy of a Future State*. In this book, Dick postulates that God lives in a physical place, which he described as "the capital of the universe." Joseph Smith may have incorporated this idea into the Book of Abraham when he introduced the idea that God resides near a star called Kolob. The relevant passage from the Book of Abraham reads:

> And I saw the stars, that they were very great, and that one of them was nearest unto the throne of God; and there were many great ones which were near unto it; And the Lord said unto me: These are the governing ones; and the name of the great one is Kolob, because it is near unto me, for I am the Lord thy God: I have set this one to govern all those which belong to the same order as that upon which thou standest. (Abraham 3:2–3).

The notion that God lives near a particular star is pretty far out there. It's so weird that it is rarely discussed in Mormon circles these days. We're willing to bet there are thousands of converts to Mormonism who attend church regularly who have never heard of Kolob. It's one of those teachings the church is quietly trying to sweep under the rug. However, if you were raised in Utah or are a Mormon of Mitt Romney's generation, you know all about Kolob. There is a song in the Mormon hymnal that wistfully imagines an interstellar trip to Kolob. A series of beautiful canyons in Zion National Park are named after Kolob. It was also the name of the Osmonds' record company in the 1970s.

No one knows where Kolob is. The Book of Abraham offers no guidance on where to point your telescope. A favorite theory among amateur Mormon theologians is that Kolob is at the very center of the Milky Way galaxy, but LDS leaders haven't spoken on the matter. We are led to believe that the planet God lives on, which presumably orbits Kolob, takes one thousand years to rotate on its axis, and this constitutes one day for God, who apparently reckons time using the rotation and orbit of this planet in much the same way as we do with earth.

Are you scratching your head in disbelief? We suspect Kolob is probably the single weirdest doctrine of Mormonism, which is why it is so often ridiculed. The comedian Bill Maher often makes fun of Mitt Romney by implying that Mitt believes in

Kolob. We've already mentioned that Kolob is a punch line in a hit Broadway musical. But is the Mormon belief in Kolob really all that weird?

We assert that Kolob sounds weird to most people because it is so unfamiliar to them. But many Christians believe things just as strange and just as demonstrably false as Joseph's translation of the Book of Abraham or the existence of the great star Kolob. For instance, lots of Christians believe that every animal on earth can trace its lineage back to a boat that survived a worldwide flood forty-five hundred years ago. Many others believe that the earth is only six thousand years old and that dinosaurs and humans walked the earth together. Looking at it objectively, these things are just as silly and absurd as the notion that God lives near a star called Kolob.

So, yes, we may soon have a president who believes that God lives on a glorified, celestial planet that orbits the great star Kolob. But that's no more alarming or consequential to us than the idea that George W. Bush probably believes in Noah's Ark.

suggestions for further reading

For an introduction to the Book of Abraham and Joseph Smith's Egyptian papyri (complete with a full-color reproduction) see Charles M. Larson, *By His Own Hand Upon Papyrus: A New Look at the Joseph Smith Papyri* (Institute for Religious Research, 1992).

CHAPTER TEN

Do Mormons believe men can become Gods? (And that God was once a man?)

the soundbite

Everyone knows Mitt Romney is ambitious. His quest for success in business has made him extraordinarily wealthy, and now he's vying for a turn as the most powerful man on earth. But these ambitions are small potatoes compared to his ultimate goal. Mitt Romney hopes to become a god one day. Indeed, all believing Mormons are striving for godhood.

the details

Most Mormons have never heard of a man named King Follett. But when Joseph Smith spoke at Follett's funeral just weeks before Joseph's own untimely death, he expounded a series of doctrines that set Mormonism apart from every other Christian faith and have prompted cries of heresy from pastors and priests of nearly every denomination ever since. In his eulogy, Joseph proclaimed that God was once a mortal man living on an earth like ours. Through his worthiness and obedience to gospel principles, he became increasingly sanctified and holy, progressing in knowledge and glory until he arrived at the point of perfection and became a god, complete with the power to create stars and planets and everything on them. Joseph also taught that we are following in God's footsteps. We are on the same mortal journey, and each of us has the potential to become gods ourselves. Thus, the highest realm of Mormon heaven – or what Latter-day Saints call the state of "exaltation" – means becoming a divine being like the creator of this world, with the same power and glory he has. The temple ceremony, which we described in chapter 5, is essentially a blueprint for how a person transforms himself from human to god. (We used the pronoun "himself" on purpose here. We'll get to the gendered nature of exaltation momentarily.) In the Doctrine and Covenants, a book of Mormon scripture, we are told faithful Mormons who keep the covenants they make in the temple "shall ... be gods, because they have all power and the angels are subject unto them." The LDS prophet Lorenzo Snow summarized this doctrine, known among Mormons as "eternal progression," with a short couplet that every Mormon of Mitt Romney's generation knows by heart: "As man is, God once was. As God is, man may become." (Again, the masculine noun is used for a reason ...)

This doctrine raises a number of interesting questions. For instance, if Mormons believe God the Father was once a man, doesn't that also mean he had to have a Heavenly Father who was his god? It stands to reason that he did. Does the doctrine of eternal progression mean Mormons are polytheists? That one is complicated. Since they don't worship God's god, or any of the other gods in the universe that have progressed to godhood, they are technically henotheists. A henotheist acknowledges the existence of many gods, but worships only one. Henotheism was common in the ancient world, but is less so today. However, since Mormons also believe Jesus and God the Father are distinct personages and both are divine, they *are* polytheists of sorts, since Father, Son, and Holy Ghost are three separate gods.

Eternal progression is one of Mormonism's most provocative teachings, and it is the target of relentless attacks by Evangelical critics. In the early eighties, an anti-Mormon ministry headed by ex-Mormon Ed Decker produced a documentary film entitled *The*

Godmakers. The film characterizes eternal progression as a satanic heresy. This film was shown widely in Utah and throughout the western United States upon release. It was among the first media productions to reveal the particulars of the temple ceremony. As a teenager, one of your authors (Phillips) skipped worship services with his family one Sunday to see a screening of the film at a Pentecostal church in Brigham City, Utah. It was a harrowing experience. With the benefit of decades of hindsight, we can now assert that the movie is sensationalistic, unfair, and grossly inaccurate in parts. (You can see it on YouTube if you have the urge.) Nevertheless, *The Godmakers* ushered in a new brand of vitriolic criticism of Mormonism that set the tone for interfaith relations in Utah, and the principal polemic, as the film's title suggests, was a diatribe assailing Joseph Smith's radical notion that humans can become gods.

In recent decades, some LDS leaders have backed away from the audacious teachings of Joseph Smith in the King Follett discourse. These days, many church authorities prefer to say that exalted Mormons will become "like God" rather than baldly proclaiming that they will be gods. This shift is designed to deflect the criticism of outspoken opponents of Mormonism like Ed Decker. We have heard anecdotal reports that eternal progression is rarely discussed in church meetings and religious instruction classes anymore. Even when we were young it was not commonly discussed from the pulpit and was considered one of the church's more esoteric teachings. When Mormons talk about exaltation, they are more likely to talk about living in God's presence or reuniting with their extended family than they are about creating worlds or performing other godlike functions. Mormons talk a lot about residing forever in a "celestial kingdom," but much less about what they'll be doing there. For this reason, we suspect some converts to Mormonism have never been given a straight introduction to the doctrine of eternal progression, even though it is still pretty plainly spelled out in

Sunday School manuals. Ultimately, we think attempting to revise the doctrine of eternal progression to make it sound less weird is going to be difficult. The words of Joseph Smith and his successors, as well as the text of the Doctrine and Covenants, are clear. Eternal progression remains central to the Mormon plan of salvation, even though members of the church sometimes describe the doctrine with euphemisms.

But if God is a man and Jesus is a man, and the Holy Ghost is always referred to as "he," what about faithful Mormon women? Recall that in an earlier chapter we wrote that marriages solemnized in Mormon temples bind husband and wife for "time and all eternity." Entering into such a "celestial marriage" is a prerequisite for entering the celestial kingdom, where, Joseph Smith taught, men become gods. If men become gods, it stands to reason that their eternal companions are goddesses, and this is the apparent destiny of righteous Mormon women.

The role of goddesses in Mormon theology is not well developed. Mormon leaders have long taught that God has a wife, and some nineteenth-century authorities even asserted that he was a polygamist. Mormons are taught through lessons and hymns that they have a Heavenly Mother who is the wife of their Heavenly Father and that she loves us just as he does. However, this Heavenly Mother appears to have no role whatsoever in human affairs. There is no mention of her being involved in the creation of the world. She has never appeared to anyone. Praying to her is forbidden, and she is not worshipped. In some respects, her role is the supernatural reflection of the archetypal Mormon wife here on earth – she stays home and manages the domestic sphere while her husband is out working. It's just that in this case, "work" involves creating galaxies, performing miracles, and giving instruction to prophets.

The invisibility of Heavenly Mother is not lost on Mormon feminists. Some LDS feminist scholars have criticized the church for ignoring the goddess and have tried to push the church to recognize her role in the plan of salvation. This kind of advocacy has sometimes been countered with ecclesiastical sanctions and censure, and in one famous case a BYU professor was fired for advocating the worship of Heavenly Mother. God's wife may be perfected and divine, but there is no indication that Heavenly Mother is ready to step out of the celestial kitchen any time soon. We're not sure how Ann Romney feels about that, but we do know that if Mitt Romney believes what he was taught in Sunday School, then being president of the United States is simply a prelude for the real power he hopes to wield after he dies. Mitt Romney, like most other active Mormons, is striving to become a god.

suggestions for further reading

For a scholarly discussion of the Mormon concept of God, see Kurt Widmer, *Mormonism and the Nature of God: A Theological Evolution, 1830–1915* (McFarland & Company, 2000). For a discussion of Heavenly Mother, see Janice Allred, *God the Mother and Other Theological Essays* (Signature Books, 1997).

CHAPTER ELEVEN

Do Mormons believe Jesus and Satan are brothers?

the soundbite

In the Republican primaries leading up to the 2008 election, Mike Huckabee, a former Baptist minister, took a shot at Mitt Romney by impugning one of the tenets of the Mormon faith. In an interview with the *New York Times Magazine*, he asked a very leading rhetorical question about Mitt's religion: "Don't Mormons believe that Jesus and the devil are brothers?" Of course, he knew the answer. They do. But what does this mean? Is this something that should concern us?

the details

Mormons do believe Jesus and Satan are siblings. But this doctrine isn't particularly strange or jarring when situated in the context of LDS theology. In order to understand this belief, it's necessary to go back – way, way back – to a time before the earth was formed. Mormons believe that before the creation of the world, all of us lived together with God in a premortal existence, probably on his planet near Kolob (see chapter 9). We were all his spirit children, but we lacked something he had – a glorified, physical body of flesh and bone. This corporeal body was something God presumably acquired when he was a mortal man on a world like ours (see chapter 10). Because God loves us, he wanted us to be able to come down to earth, receive a body, and have an opportunity to advance to godhood like him.

A grand council was convened in heaven, and all of us attended. The purpose of the council was to devise a plan that would allow us to acquire bodies, go through the process of mortality, and receive the necessary ordinances to facilitate re-entry into God's kingdom and ultimately progress to godhood, where we would enjoy the same glory and power as our Father in Heaven.

Two of the most intelligent and powerful of God's spirit children came forward with plans. The first was Lucifer, who became the devil. Lucifer told God he would oversee all life on earth, and would force humans to obey God's commandments. He would make the saving ordinances of the gospel mandatory, and by forcing us to behave, not a single soul would be lost. Every one of us would return to God to receive divine glory. In exchange for pulling off this great feat, Lucifer wanted all of the glory and credit for redeeming the souls of humankind for himself.

An alternative plan was presented by Heavenly Father's firstborn spirit child, Jesus. The premortal Jesus proposed that all the spirits must go to earth and find their own way back to God through choosing obedience to the precepts of the gospel. No one would be forced to obey, and everyone would have to earn his or her place in the celestial kingdom. However, in order to make things easier, the premortal Jesus offered to go to earth himself at a specified time in order to provide an example to his spirit siblings, and to offer himself as a sacrifice for all the mistakes we were certain to make as we journeyed through life. Some would make it back, and some would fail, but all would rise and fall based on their merits. Most importantly, the premortal Jesus wanted none of the credit for implementing his plan, and offered all glory and honor to the Father.

By now you have probably figured out which plan prevailed. God liked his firstborn son's plan best and decided that rather than cede any glory to Lucifer, it would be better to risk the loss of all of his children by following the course prescribed by the premortal Jesus. This did not sit well with Lucifer, nor with the billions of God's spirit children who sided with him. Rather than admit defeat, he and his followers, who constituted a third of the premortal spirits, launched a civil war in heaven. No one knows how long the battle raged, but Lucifer eventually lost, and he and all his followers were cast out of heaven. These rebellious spirits will never have a body, and they will never be able to return to God's presence. They are doomed to reside in a place Mormons call "outer darkness."

When we were kids in Sunday school, this story made perfect sense to us. Now, however, we find it hard to imagine that an omniscient being who loves his children would ever act this way. For one thing, if God knows everything, he already knows which of his spirit children are going to return to him and which will fail. This makes the "plan" nothing more than a charade. You may think you have free will, but you're really only free to do what God already knows you're going to do. What you call free will, God calls ignorance. There are other logical problems and theological pitfalls associated with this story as well, but we'll leave it to you to work through them. Suffice it to say that Mormonism has a very different take on the classic "problem of evil" that has plagued Christian theologians for centuries, because Mormon ideas about the nature of Satan and Jesus are very different from those of mainstream Christianity – which leads us back to where this chapter began.

Mormons believe that since Jesus and Lucifer are spirit children of our Heavenly Father, they are literally siblings. But every person that has ever lived on earth is also a spirit child of Heavenly Father, which makes us all siblings and members of the same gargantuan dysfunctional family. Lucifer is Jesus's brother, but he is also your brother. Jesus is your brother as well. In fact, Mormons often refer to Jesus as "our elder brother," an affectionate term that references social relations in the premortal life.

They refer to one another as "brother" and "sister" for the same reason. So, in sum, Jesus and Satan are siblings in the same way that any human that has ever lived is the brother or sister of any other human that has ever lived. Mike Huckabee's offhand question makes it seem like Jesus and Satan are the Mormon version of yin and yang, or Romulus and Remus. The truth, however, is much more banal.

suggestions for further reading

The story of the war in heaven and the role of Jesus and Satan in Mormon theology are discussed in Charles R. Harrell's *This Is My Doctrine: The Development of Mormon Theology* (Greg Kofford Books, 2011).

CHAPTER TWELVE

Who goes to Mormon heaven?

the soundbite

The Mormon afterlife is more complicated than the orthodox Christian afterlife. It is also more merciful. For most Christians, when you die you either go to heaven or you burn forever in hell. But for Mormons, there are several different places you can end up, based partly on what you do and partly on what you believe. What do Mormons believe about the afterlife, and who goes to Mormon heaven?

the details

The earliest Mormon beliefs about the afterlife were pretty similar to those espoused by the major religious denominations of the time. The Book of Mormon presents a view of salvation and damnation that is familiar to most Christians: the righteous dwell in the presence of God in heaven, and the wicked burn in hell forever. But as an inveterate theological innovator, Joseph Smith was not content simply to import standard Christian doctrine into his new faith. As his prophetic career progressed, Joseph developed a concept of the afterlife that was complex, nuanced, and addressed a number of vexing questions about heaven and hell that were controversial in his day.

According to Mormon theology, when people die, their soul immediately goes to one of two places. Mormons who were obedient to the teachings of the church will head to the Mormon version of paradise. Mormon paradise is a place of happiness, but it is also bustling with activity, as we shall soon see. Those who don't end up in paradise go to "spirit prison." Spirit prison gets its name from a verse in the New Testament (1 Peter 3:19), which states that after his death Jesus traveled to a "prison" to make a proclamation to the spirits of those who drowned in the Noachian flood. This verse is notoriously difficult for biblical scholars, and even Martin Luther admitted he had no clue what Peter meant. Joseph Smith taught that the spirit prison housed those who had rejected the gospel or broken the commandments in this life. Those people were despondent over their sins and were in a condition that some Mormon theologians have described as hell. Thus, the spirit prison isn't a place with bars and cells, but rather a place where people are imprisoned by shame and regret.

The spirit prison also houses those who never had the chance to hear the Mormon message while they were alive. This constitutes the vast majority of people throughout history, and most people on the earth today. According to LDS theology, no one can return to live with God without having received certain gospel ordinances, so these spirits cannot enter paradise. However, since their ignorance of the gospel is not their fault, they will have an opportunity to hear the gospel in spirit prison and accept (or reject) ordinances performed on their behalf in Mormon temples. Even as you read this, missionaries from paradise are busy canvassing the spirit prison, seeking and teaching prospective converts just as their earthly counterparts are doing. Those who accept Mormonism in the spirit prison and receive their vicarious ordinances can then enter paradise. Jesus apparently kicked off this missionary effort by visiting those who died in the flood.

Paradise and the spirit prison are only temporary abodes. When Jesus returns to earth after the apocalypse, the spirits in paradise will be resurrected, and they will live on earth during Christ's millennial reign. Those who remain in the spirit prison must wait a thousand years before they are resurrected. When the thousand years are finished, everyone will stand before God for the final judgment. It is then that people will be sent to their eternal destinations.

In Christendom, the final judgment determines who goes to heaven and who goes to hell. But in Mormonism, there are gradations in heaven, and there is nothing like the Christian hell. No one knows exactly where Joseph Smith got his ideas about the afterlife, but he was influenced by something Paul wrote in his first epistle to the Corinthians (see I Corinthians 15:40–42). Based on his interpretation of this passage, Joseph taught that heaven had three kingdoms, or "degrees of glory," which he identified as the "celestial," the "terrestrial," and the "telestial." The glory of the celestial kingdom is compared to the luminescence of the sun. By comparison, the terrestrial kingdom shines like the moon, and the telestial kingdom is like twinkling stars in the night sky.

The telestial kingdom is the final destination of the wicked. Unless they were converted in spirit prison, Adolf Hitler will be there, as well as Pol Pot and Joseph Stalin. All of the unrepentant murderers, adulterers, liars, thieves, and pedophiles will be there too. But the telestial kingdom is not like the Christian hell. There is no fire and brimstone, and Satan and his angels are not present. The telestial kingdom is a part of heaven. In fact, Mormon scriptures declare that the telestial kingdom has a glory "which surpasses all understanding." According to a common Mormon folk doctrine – based loosely on something Joseph Smith purportedly said – this lesser heaven is so marvelous that if you could glimpse it, you would kill yourself to get there (because that's where people who commit suicide end up).

Other folk understandings of the telestial kingdom are also common among Mormons. Some say that the endowment ceremony implies that the earth is currently in a telestial state and that those who inherit the telestial kingdom live in a place that is like this earth, where peace and tranquility exist alongside tribulation and strife. Still others see the telestial kingdom as a place of mental anguish. The inhabitants of the telestial kingdom are denied the presence of Jesus and God the Father, and they are constantly reminded of how they have fallen short. According to this view, even though it is not a place of physical punishment, the telestial kingdom is a kind of hell.

The terrestrial kingdom – the heaven in the middle – is where good people who aren't Mormons end up. We suspect you'll find Ghandi there, as well as Martin Luther King and Mother Teresa. This is also where Mormons who weren't assiduous in keeping the commandments go. Many Mormons compare the terrestrial kingdom to the Garden of Eden: a beautiful, idyllic utopia. The presence of Jesus is felt in the terrestrial kingdom, but the fullness of God the Father is absent.

The apex of Mormon heaven is the celestial kingdom. This kingdom is reserved for Mormons who have made covenants in the temple and remained true to the teachings of the church. Little children who die before they are old enough to be responsible for their sins go here as well. (There is no concept of original sin in Mormonism.) The heirs to the celestial kingdom enjoy the presence of both Jesus and God the Father. This kingdom is subdivided into three parts. The highest realm is called exaltation, and it is here that men and women become gods and goddesses and create their own worlds.

Some scholars have argued that Joseph Smith's tripartite heaven was designed as a compromise between the competing theological views of his day. On the one hand, proponents of universal salvation argued that since God was merciful and had a perfect love for his creation, he would ultimately admit everyone into heaven, regardless of what they had done. On the other hand, itinerant clergy who were active in Joseph Smith's community were adamant that God's judgments were awesome and final and sinners would get what they deserved. By imagining degrees of glory, Joseph preserved the notion that people were judged on their merits, while rejecting the idea that a merciful, loving God would subject his children to eternal torture.

But if everyone goes to some sort of heaven, where does the devil end up? There is actually one more destination in the Mormon afterlife. It is called "outer darkness," and it is the place where the devil and his angels will spend eternity, cut off from the presence of God forever. It is also the place where the "sons of perdition" will go. In order to be a son (or presumably daughter) of perdition, you would have to have a perfect knowledge of the truthfulness of the gospel and then deny and repudiate it. Sons of perdition are a special class of sinners, and according to Mormon theology, Cain is the only confirmed son of perdition we know of (although most Mormons think Judas Iscariot fits the bill as well).

In sum, Mormon heaven is a complicated place, and many aspects of the afterlife are poorly defined in LDS theology. The concepts of "heaven" and "hell" have very different connotations in Mormonism, and aside from the devil and his angels, virtually no one ends up in a place of eternal punishment.

suggestions for further reading

The ins and outs of Mormon heaven are discussed in Charles R. Harrell, *This Is My Doctrine: The Development of Mormon Theology* (Greg Kofford Books, 2011). A classic discourse on the three degrees of glory delivered by Mormon apostle Melvin J. Ballard can be found online here: http://www.shields-research.org/General/LDS_Leaders/Q12/Ballard_Melvin_J/01Three_Degrees_cap400x100.pdf

CHAPTER THIRTEEN

Do Mormons believe in the Bible?

the soundbite

If Mitt Romney is elected president of the United States this fall, he will take the oath of office with his hand on the Bible. Like most Christians, Mormons believe that the Bible is divinely inspired. They quote the Bible in worship services and read it for guidance. But LDS views of scripture are quite different from those of other denominations. Mormons believe in an "open canon" and claim that revelation and instruction from heaven continues unabated. Throughout the history of the church, Mormon prophets have recorded these revelations and presented them to the church as scripture. Thus, Mormons have additional scripture they accept as authoritative and inspired. In their view, these augment and amplify their understanding of the Bible.

the details

Mormonism was founded on the idea of continuing revelation. The notion that instruction and knowledge were still being imparted through inspiration from God was one of the essential selling points of the new religion. Joseph Smith was different from ordinary pastors and preachers; he claimed to be a prophet like Isaiah and Ezekiel of old. Rather than interpret the scriptures, he received new scripture for his followers. He touted the Book of Mormon as evidence that God was still revealing his word to humankind. It was a message that resonated with the citizens of the antebellum mid-Atlantic and Western Reserve, and Joseph's fledgling church attracted many followers.

As the self-proclaimed mouthpiece of God, Joseph Smith recorded scores of revelations. He dictated revelations to disseminate doctrine, settle disputes among his followers, and get church members to do things they were reluctant to do. Many of Joseph's revelations are compiled into books of Mormon scripture, and together with the Book of Mormon, these constitute the official Mormon canon. Altogether, this canon consists of:

> *The Book of Mormon* – This book recounts the history and teachings of ancient prophets from Israel who traveled to the Americas and built their civilizations here from about 600 BCE to roughly 400 CE. It is the first of Joseph's canonical works and the one that launched his career as a frontier prophet. It is written in a style that mimics the 1611 King James Version of the Bible, complete with "thees" and "thous." Mark Twain famously referred to the Book of Mormon as "chloroform in print," and we think he was being charitable. The book has a banal, repetitive plot. The prose is stilted and verbose. The phrase "and it came to pass ..." is used 1,297 times as a device to advance the narrative.
>
> Scholars have argued that one function of the Book of Mormon was to settle some of the vexing doctrinal disputes of Joseph Smith's day. Debates over original sin, infant baptism, predestination, and the role of scripture are all discussed in its pages. The Book of Mormon represents the earliest form of Mormon theology, and as Joseph Smith's prophetic career progressed he abandoned many of its teachings. No extant discourse or missive of Joseph Smith quotes the Book of Mormon.
>
> *The Doctrine and Covenants* – This book of scripture is a compilation of revelations received by Joseph Smith and a few of his successsors. Most of the revelations are written in the first

person, with God himself doing the talking. It is in the Doctrine and Covenants that many of the distinctive doctrines of Mormonism – like polygamy and the tripartite heaven – are revealed. Many of the revelations in the present edition of the Doctrine and Covenants have been heavily redacted from their original form, raising questions about how much of the wording in the revelations Joseph regarded as direct from God and how much he saw as his own.

The Pearl of Great Price – This is the shortest and most esoteric book of LDS scripture. It contains the Book of Moses, which presents additional information to supplement the book of Genesis. It also contains the Book of Abraham, which we discuss at length in chapter 9. The Pearl of Great Price also includes a short autobiography of Joseph Smith that recounts the visions and heavenly manifestations that led to the organization of the church.

Mormons are often criticized for having books of scripture other than the Bible. The church's expanded canon is one reason why Evangelical Christians accuse Mormonism of being a counterfeit or heretical version of Christianity. But other Christian churches approach the canon in varying ways as well. For instance, Catholics and Orthodox Christians regard the intertestamental Apocrypha as fully canonical, so they have "extra" scripture too. We often encounter students in our classes who completely disregard the Old Testament whenever they encounter something in its pages that disturbs them. When they read about massacres committed at God's command or about repressive social practices like patriarchy and slavery, or about God's penchant for levying the death penalty for trivial offenses like working on the Sabbath or talking back to one's parents, they wave it off with a flippant phrase like, "Yeah, but that's in the Old Testament." While they may give lip service to the historicity and inspiration of the Old Testament, they clearly do not feel bound by it.

In a strange way, Mormons are even less bound by what they read in the Bible than our students are. One of the church's Articles of Faith states: "We believe the Bible to be the word of God *as far as it is translated correctly* . . ." The italicized part is important, because it highlights a distinction between Mormons and other conservative Christians. Mormons reject the doctrine of Biblical inerrancy. They acknowledge that scribal errors and interpolations have corrupted the original text of the Bible. In this sense, the Mormon view of the Old and New Testaments accords with the findings of modern Biblical scholars. Most Mormons believe that some books of scripture were excluded from the Bible for political reasons and some books that made it in are less useful than others. For example, Joseph Smith denounced the Song of Solomon as uninspired and argued that it had no place in the canon.

Toward the end of his life, Joseph Smith began editing the Bible, ostensibly restoring the text through revelation to its original meaning before the errors and interpolations crept in. Known as the Joseph Smith Translation, Mormon authorities and theologians occasionally quote from it, but it is not canonical for Mormons. This is probably because it was a work in progress when Joseph was assassinated. Some scholars also maintain that it is difficult to know whether Joseph believed he was reinstating the primordial Greek and Hebrew text or simply adding commentary.

In sum, if Mitt Romney gets a chance to put his hand on the Bible and swear an oath to uphold the Constitution, he will likely take it very seriously. Like all devout Mormons, Mitt Romney believes the Bible to be the word of God. But his view of the Bible is a little more nuanced than some Evangelicals in the Republican Party are probably comfortable with. And he'd likely take the oath just as seriously if his hand were placed on the Book of Mormon instead.

suggestions for further reading

The definitive study of Mormon views on scripture is Philip L. Barlow's *Mormons and the Bible: The Place of the Latter-day Saints in American Religion* (Oxford University Press, 1997).

Part IV: Social Issues

What do Mormons think about feminism?

What do Mormons think about abortion?

What do Mormons think about homosexuality?

Are Mormons racist?

CHAPTER FOURTEEN

What do Mormons think about feminism?

the soundbite

Since marrying Mitt Romney, Ann Romney hasn't worked for pay outside the home. She's been a stay-at-home mom, and as first lady of Massachusetts she became involved in charitable work and helped with Mitt's faith-based initiatives. Ann's domestic and charitable work closely fits the role her church would prescribe for her. The Mormon church is big on stay-at-home moms and promotes the idea that the economic and political sphere is men's work. That may seem anachronistic by 2012 standards, but Mormonism has always had a controversial stance on gender issues. What is the status of women in the LDS church?

the details

Like most conservative Christian denominations, Mormonism is a patriarchal religion. A patriarchal system is one where men are dominant and women are subordinate. Women in the LDS church are not allowed to hold the lay priesthood, for which all men and boys over the age of twelve are eligible. There have never been any female members of the governing hierarchy, and we're not holding our breath waiting for that to change. In Mormon temples, women take an oath to obey their husbands, while the husbands take an oath to obey God. Each participant in the temple endowment receives a secret temple name. Husbands know their wife's secret name, but wives are not permitted to know their husband's. At the end of days, when men are resurrected, they will use their wife's secret temple name to call her out of the grave. Some early church leaders taught that unless a husband calls his wife out of the earth, she will miss the resurrection of the righteous and remain in the ground until the "steerage class" resurrection that takes place later.

In the past, women have been admonished not to work outside the home and to relegate their labors to the domestic sphere. This is still the ideal within the church, but the exigencies of modern life means that female labor force participation among LDS women is not much different than the national average. Couples have been told not to limit the size of their families, and some church leaders have disparaged birth control, although its use is not prohibited. Mormons have followed this advice, and their families tend to be larger than the national average. Demographically speaking, Utah is the youngest state in the union and has been for decades, owing to very high birth rates among the Latter-day Saints.

The Mormon church was vehemently opposed to the Equal Rights Amendment to the constitution and mobilized against it. Some proponents of the ERA within the church were even excommunicated, although their support for the amendment wasn't the sole reason why. Female professors at BYU have been fired for their feminist activism, and the powerful president of the quorum of the twelve apostles has stated that feminists (along with scholars and homosexuals) pose a grave threat to the church.

In spite of this, the church continues to stress that it teaches that men and women are fundamentally equal. In "The Family: A Proclamation to the World" – an encyclical on gender and family roles published and disseminated by the Mormon hierarchy in 1995, the church hierarchy asserts:

> By divine design, fathers are to preside over their families in

love and righteousness and are responsible to provide the necessities of life and protection for their families. Mothers are primarily responsible for the nurture of their children. In these sacred responsibilities, fathers and mothers are obligated to help one another as equal partners.

Of course, the church's brand of gender equality is of the "separate but equal" variety, and we all know how well that works. Indeed, when read carefully, the quote starkly contradicts itself. The first sentence declares that men preside over their families. We could quibble over what "preside" means, but according to the Merriam-Webster Dictionary, it means "to occupy the place of authority." In other words, men are the ultimate authority in Mormon families, and that's the way God wants it. Men might be enjoined to be benevolent rulers of the household, but they rule nonetheless. While men are bringing home the bacon and ruling the roost, women are responsible for raising the kids.

If you think this sounds like the 1950s, it might be because the Mormon hierarchy is a gerontocracy comprised of men who came of age in the 1950s. Sociological data suggest that this view of the family is anachronistic and unrealistic in 2012. Only seven percent of American families (using the census definition of families) comprise a man in the labor force and a stay-at-home mom with kids. Of course, Mitt and Ann Romney fall within that seven percent, and we hope we aren't being presumptuous when we assume that their vast wealth had something to do with making this arrangement possible. The rest of America (and, frankly, most Mormons) live in different familial circumstances: single-parent homes, dual-earner homes, same-sex partnerships, etc. Statistically speaking, the odds that a household conforms to the traditional, idealized Mormon family norm are about the same as the odds that they will own a Nissan.

Of course, many Mormons will respond by claiming that raising children is an awesome responsibility and stay-at-home moms deserve our respect. They'll get no argument from us on that. We wish more women – and men – had the option of leaving the labor force to spend time with their young children. Mormons will also claim that women *do* serve in leadership positions in the church, including church-wide administrative posts. This is true, but women cannot call other women to leadership positions; they can only rise to their administrative posts if they are appointed by a man. Moreover, the jobs that women do in the church put them in positions of authority only over other women and children. In the church's ecclesiastical flow chart, no woman has authority over any adult man. Moreover, the highest echelons of church leadership are closed off to women. No woman can be an apostle, let alone a prophet.

Nevertheless, despite the church's patriarchal governance style, rank-and-file members of the church have views on a woman's place in society that don't seem to differ much from those of the rest of the country. Even though the church teaches that women should stay home with the kids, survey research shows that only one in five Mormons disapprove of women working outside the home. That's not far off the national average. However, Mormons are much more likely to say that when a woman with young children works outside the home, the kids will suffer. About one in four members of the church – slightly more than the national average – think women are not temperamentally suited for politics. But ninety-five percent say they would vote for a qualified female candidate for president.

Much has been written lately about the "gender gap" in American politics. As we're writing this, polls show that women favor President Obama over Mitt Romney by a wide margin. We're not sure if Mitt's Mormonism contributes to women's reservations about supporting him. But the internals of these polls show that the women Mormonism marginalizes, feminists and career women, are the least likely to vote for Mitt. Of course, they're the least likely to vote for any Republican, so this may be another case where Mormonism and the conservative agenda are in sync.

suggestions for further reading

An excellent study of Utah women that covers the LDS church's encounter with the feminist movement and the Equal Rights Amendment is Martha Sonntag Bradley's *Pedestals and Podiums: Utah Women, Religious Authority, and Equal Rights* (Signature Books, 2005). For a journalistic account of the how Mormon women see their role in the church and society, see Dorothy Allred Solomon, *The Sisterhood: Inside the Lives of Mormon Women* (Palgrave Macmillan, 2007).

CHAPTER FIFTEEN

What do Mormons think about abortion?

the soundbite

In his bid to become governor of Massachusetts, Mitt Romney repeatedly asserted that he would support and defend a woman's right to choose. When he ran for president in 2008, he had a change of heart and supported the Republican Party platform that would have outlawed abortion. Mitt Romney has clearly changed his position with respect to abortion, but the church he belongs to has had a consistent position on it throughout Mitt's political career. What do Mormons think about abortion?

the details

The Church of Jesus Christ of Latter-day Saints condemns elective abortion. Anyone who has, performs, or facilitates an abortion is subject to church discipline, including excommunication. However, there are circumstances under which the church might consider an abortion justified. These include: rape, incest, the life or health of the mother, or if the baby has birth defects and cannot survive outside the womb. Moreover, the church does not equate abortion with murder and has no official position on when a developing fetus becomes the moral equivalent of a human being. This means that the church's position on abortion is more liberal than many Evangelical churches', and – if his statements on things like "personhood" amendments are any guide – possibly more liberal than Mitt Romney's.

A woman who has had an abortion cannot join the Mormon church unless she is cleared by the appropriate ecclesiastical leader. On our missions, the mission president usually gave this clearance. However, those who have committed murder cannot join the church unless they are cleared by the first presidency – the highest echelon of Mormon leadership. This distinction is reinforced by the church's contention that abortion is a sin "like unto murder," which, of course, means that it isn't actually murder. It is important to note that the church does not require its members to support the criminalization of abortion, and hence it is possible to be a member in good standing and describe oneself as pro-choice, just as Mitt Romney did when he ran for the Senate in 1994.

The church's pro-life stance has been adopted by the rank-and-file members. According to the General Social Survey, Mormons are generally less tolerant of abortion than mainline Protestants, Catholics, or Southern Baptists. Only about 17 percent think abortion should be legal for any reason, and less than 20 percent think abortion is justified if the mother is too poor to care for the child. However, a strong majority of Mormons agree that abortion can be justified if the mother's life or health is in danger, if birth defects are present, or the pregnancy resulted from a rape.

We don't know how Mitt Romney would govern with respect to the issue of abortion. We suspect these days his views are shaped more by his party than by his church. Although the LDS view on abortion is compatible with the Republican Party's platform, the church's position on abortion is actually fairly moderate for such an otherwise conservative faith.

suggestions for further reading

There is no book-length treatment of Mormon views on abortion, but there are a number of useful scholarly articles. Tim Heaton describes Mormon attitudes toward abortion in a 1992 article in *Dialogue: A Journal of Mormon Thought*, "Demographics of the Contemporary Mormon Family" (volume 25, number 3). L. J. Conley examines Mormon childbearing practices in a 1990 article in *Neonatal Network*, "Childbearing and Childrearing Practices in Mormonism" (volume 9, number 3). Joanne Duke explores these issues at greater length in a 1985 master's thesis, *Mormon Attitudes Toward High Risk Pregnancy Management: Birth Control, Prenatal Diagnosis, and Abortion* (University of Utah).

CHAPTER SIXTEEN

What do Mormons think about homosexuality?

the soundbite

Mitt Romney used to be more supportive of gay rights than he is now. When he ran for Senate in 1994, he reached out to gay rights groups in Massachusetts asking for their vote and denounced discrimination against same-sex couples. He also courted the gay vote when he ran for governor in 2002. When Massachusetts's highest court ruled that discrimination against gay couples was illegal, he hoped to implement civil unions as a "separate-but-equal" solution, but this was not enough for the court, and gay marriage became legal in the Bay State. This didn't seem to bother Mitt much, and he didn't do anything about it. Nevertheless, Mitt has recently spoken out against civil unions and supports an amendment to the Constitution banning gay marriage. These days, he's not a very gay-friendly guy. We suspect Mitt's change of heart on gay issues is linked to his national political ambitions. The extent to which he'd pursue an anti-gay agenda if he became president is a matter of conjecture, but one thing is for sure: Mitt's church is not very gay-friendly either. What is the Mormon Church's position on homosexuality?

the details

The LDS Church's position on homosexuality has evolved over the course of a generation. In the 1970s, when the gay rights movement was just beginning, church leaders denounced homosexuality in the strongest possible terms. In his book *The Miracle of Forgiveness* – a best seller in Mormon circles – the prophet Spencer W. Kimball labeled homosexuality repugnant, degenerate, and unnatural. Apostle Bruce R. McConkie wrote that because of the spread of homosexuality, the world was as wicked as it was when God destroyed it in the time of Noah. In 1978, an article in the *LDS Church News* asked:

> On what basis do [homosexuals] demand special privilege? Who are they that they should parade their debauchery and call it clean? They even form their own churches and profess to worship the very God who denounces their behavior – and they do not repent. They form their own political groups and seek to compel the public to respect them. Do other violators of the law of God receive special consideration? Do the robbers, the thieves, the adulterers?

The church used to send gay members to quack psychiatrists practicing "reparative therapy" designed to turn them straight. These "pray-away-the-gay" methods sometimes involved shock therapy and included such measures as hooking up sensors to a person's penis. Mormon leaders also counseled gay men to begin dating women and find a wife as soon as possible. They reasoned that once a man was in his proper role, nature would take over. No one knows how many men took this advice, but first-hand accounts of the tragic results of this policy are well documented. Presumably lesbianism would have been approached similarly, though little information is available on the subject.

The Mormon church's aversion to homosexuality is rooted in its doctrine. The church teaches that gender is not something that emerges from our physical bodies. According to the church's 1995 proclamation on the family, "Gender is an essential characteristic of individual premortal, mortal, and eternal identity." Mormons believe the souls of all human beings existed before birth. In that premortal state you were either male or female. The physical body you acquired when you were born is matched to the gender you have always had, and always will have, even after death. The unspoken ramification of this is that because God didn't make any homosexual spirits, being gay is neither natural nor immutable, and it is certainly not an eternal feature of anyone's sexual identity.

LDS ideas about marriage do not accommodate homosexuality either. True salvation within Mormonism is reserved for those who are married in a Mormon temple, and since gay marriages are forbidden there, there can be no gay people in the highest realms of Mormon heaven – unless they enter into sham heterosexual marriages. Moreover, the only church-approved, God-endorsed orgasm a person can have during waking hours is one that is provided by one's spouse. No pre-marital hanky-panky and no masturbation of any kind is ever allowed. The church does not recognize the validity of gay marriage even in states or nations where it is legal, and hence gay people cannot have orgasms without committing a sin (unless a sham-marriage spouse somehow manages to get them off).

We think the vast majority of believing Mormons would agree that our description of the centrality of gender to the church's plan of salvation is accurate. These doctrines haven't changed since the church first began reacting to the increasing visibility of homosexuals in society, and they are unlikely to change any time soon. However, what has changed dramatically is the way the church now deals with its gay members. The church has disavowed "pray-away-the-gay" quackery, and it no longer counsels gay people to enter heterosexual marriages.

The church's views on the etiology of homosexuality are also in flux. While we suspect that no Mormon leader would ever entertain the notion of a gay premortal spirit, some LDS authorities have made statements suggesting they believe homosexuality might have its origin in the womb or emerge from the interplay of biology and childhood socialization. In other words, some leaders acknowledge that a sexual preference for persons of the same sex might not be a conscious choice and might not be amenable to therapy. (Although others – including the powerful president of the Twelve Apostles – suggest that it is.) For this reason, the church's current policy for dealing with gay members draws a sharp distinction between homosexual attraction and homosexual behavior. If you are a man, it is not a sin to be sexually attracted to other men, and likewise for same-sex-attracted women. However, it is a grievous sin to act on those attractions. A gay person can be a member of the church in good standing, so long as that person is celibate and refrains from all sexual activity. That doesn't sound like a good deal to us, especially considering all the churches out there that gladly embrace homosexuals as they are, but there are many gay Mormons who live this way.

Living celibate may sound hard, but the church teaches that denying homosexual urges is the same as overcoming any temptation to sin. Converts to the church who smoke must agree to give up tobacco. Overcoming an addiction to cigarettes is difficult, and it is a temptation not everyone faces, but faithful Mormons are expected to do it. Some people, because of disability or disfigurement, are unable to find mates. Even though these people have sexual urges, if they are Mormons, they cannot masturbate or visit a prostitute to satisfy them. Thus, the official position of the Mormon Church on homosexuality is that you can "feel" gay but you can't "act" gay. In practical terms, homosexuals who want to remain members of the LDS Church must be celibate and single for their entire lives.

This isn't meant to be punitive. The church thinks it is protecting people from serious sin. Protecting people from serious sin is a moral imperative, because nothing less than eternal salvation hangs in the balance. This is why Mormon leaders can make onerous demands on gay members of the church and stigmatize same-sex relationships while affirming they are acting in everyone's best interests. That is also why Mormons have been at the forefront of political and legal efforts to fight against gay marriage.

The LDS hierarchy's disdain for homosexual relations has trickled down to rank-and-file Mormons. In an important survey of social attitudes, 84 percent of Latter-day Saints agreed that homosexual sex is "always or almost always wrong." About two-thirds say they oppose gay marriage. These percentages are on par with notoriously anti-gay denominations like the Southern Baptists Convention and far exceed those for Catholics and mainline Protestant groups like the Methodists and Presbyterians.

We can't say for sure if Mitt thinks like the bulk of his co-religionists, but his statements on the campaign trail suggest he does. Still, since the Mormon position on homosexuality is fully compatible with the Republican Party platform, it's hard to say whether Mitt's anti-gay campaign rhetoric is a function of religion or politics. Maybe it's both.

suggestions for further reading

For a useful collection of essays on Mormonism and homosexuality, see Ron Schow, Wayne Schow, and Marybeth Raynes, *Peculiar People: Mormons and Same-Sex Orientation* (Signature Books, 1991). For a sociological study of gay Mormons, see Rick Phillips, *Conservative Christian Identity and Same-Sex Orientation: The Case of Gay Mormons* (Peter Lang, 2005). For a faithful Mormon's perspective on the matter, see A. Dean Byrd, *Mormons and Homosexuality* (Millenial Press, 2008).

CHAPTER SEVENTEEN

Are Mormons racist?

the soundbite

The Church of Jesus Christ of Latter-day Saints isn't the only Christian denomination trying to live down its racist past. But the LDS church's racist past is more recent, and arguably more egregious than many. Until 1978, men of African descent could not be ordained to the church's lay clergy, and no black person was allowed to participate in temple rituals. Since these rituals are essential for true salvation within Mormonism, it is reasonable to infer that until 1978, black people could not enter the highest echelon of Mormon heaven. Nevertheless, since 1978 the church has worked feverishly to expunge its racist past, and it is now a stalwart proponent of racial equality. How did the church develop its policies on race, and why did they change so abruptly?

the details

Mitt Romney's father, George Romney, was the governor of Michigan and an ardent proponent of civil rights. This did not sit well with some of the leaders of the LDS church. In 1964, George received a letter from Mormon apostle Delbert Stapley. In the letter, Stapley outlined his opposition to civil rights legislation, stating that "the Negro is entitled to considerations . . . but not full social benefits or inter-marriage privileges with the Whites, nor should the Whites be forced to accept them into restricted White areas." He argued that "negroes" were cursed by God and implored George to rethink his position and to bring it in line with what Stapley perceived to be the doctrine of the church. To his credit, George Romney ignored the apostle's advice and continued to support civil rights. Stapley's views are shocking by today's standards, but they were probably fairly standard for old conservative white guys in 1964. Stapley's ideas had been shaped by over a century of Mormon theology and policy dealing with the subject of race.

The Church of Jesus Christ of Latter-day Saints has a racist past. That's not saying much, of course, because many Christian denominations in the United States have a deplorable record on race relations. The nation's largest Protestant denomination – the Southern Baptist Convention – has acknowledged its role in the subjugation of African Americans in a lengthy official *mea culpa* released in 1995. Southern Baptists believed Blacks were the descendants of Noah's grandson Canaan, whose lineage was condemned to lives of servitude because Ham, Canaan's father and Noah's son, saw the patriarch Noah lying drunk and naked in his tent. Bible scholars have long been stumped by this bizarre passage in Genesis chapter 9. But while what happened in the tent is unknown, it is pretty clear that Noah cursed Ham's son Canaan and decreed that his progeny would be slaves because of the incident.

The origins of the myths that justify Mormon racist policies are harder to pin down. The historical record shows that in the earliest days of the church, people of African descent were sometimes ordained to the lay clergy, known among Mormons as the priesthood. The first black person known to have held the priesthood was a man named Elijah Abel. Abel was born a slave and joined the church in 1832. He served as a missionary and later followed Brigham Young to Utah. Under Joseph Smith, the Mormons evolved into abolitionists, and their anti-slavery leanings were one source of friction with their neighbors. Just before his death, Joseph ran for president of the United States. He advocated the end of slavery, proposed compensating slaveholders for their losses, and wanted to establish a separate territory for former slaves. He also taught that slaves could join the church, but only with the permission of their masters. Thus, in its earliest incarnation, Mormonism was somewhat more accommodating to blacks than in subsequent generations, and Joseph's political views on racial issues were progressive for his day, at least toward the end of his life.

But it's important not to get carried away with Joseph's late-life views. Despite his abolitionist proclivities and his willingness to ordain at least some black men to the priesthood, Joseph still held noxious theological ideas about race. For instance, he taught that people of African stock were the cursed descendants of the first murderer, Cain. According to Mormon scripture, dark skin was the visible mark of this curse, causing Cain's progeny to be "despised among all people." Sometime after the ordination of Elijah Abel and before the publication of the Book of Abraham, Joseph seems to have developed the idea that the actual curse (as opposed to the mark of the curse) was a prohibition against holding the priesthood – something that is essential for true salvation within Mormonism. While Southern Baptists argued that Ham's descendants had been cursed with slavery through his son Canaan, Joseph wrote that Ham's wife was a descendant of Cain who preserved the cursed lineage by bringing it on the ark, and according to the book of Abraham, Ham was "cursed … as pertaining to the Priesthood."

The notion that dark skin was the mark of a curse and not the curse itself was a refinement of Joseph's views on skin pigment. You may recall from chapter 3 that Joseph taught that Native Americans were similarly branded with dark skin, which made them "loathsome" and "filthy." However, in the Book of Mormon, where this teaching appears, dark skin does not signify a deeper curse, but is the curse itself. The church has never prohibited Native Americans from holding the priesthood or participating in temple rituals. One Mormon prophet even taught that Native Americans who joined the church and kept the commandments would eventually have the curse lifted and turn white.

Assessing Joseph Smith's views on race in the context of antebellum Missouri and southern Illinois is difficult. It's hard to give him a pass, but he was, as they say, a man of his time. However, when the bulk of the Mormons migrated to Utah after his death, the unambiguously racist policies of the church he founded began to take shape. The Utah territory was formed in 1850, and part of Congress's logic in setting territorial boundaries was to preserve a balance between free and slave states. Technically, at the time the territory was formed, Utah would have been free to choose whether to be a free or slave state upon admission to the union. This made slavery a hot-button issue even in the sparsely populated western desert. It may also have given Brigham Young political reasons for formalizing a policy that prohibited blacks from being ordained to the priesthood. This policy remained in place until 1978.

It is unlikely that Young lost much sleep over the policy. He was not shy about his racist views, and unlike his predecessor, his sentiments were neither nuanced nor abstruse. For instance, he advocated "death on the spot" for miscegenation. In a speech recorded in an important compendium of Mormon discourses, Young declared:

> You see some classes of the human family that are black, uncouth, uncomely, disagreeable and low in their habits, wild, and seemingly deprived of nearly all the blessings of the intelligence that is generally bestowed upon mankind. The first man that committed the odious crime of killing one of his brethren will be cursed the longest of any one of the children of Adam. Cain slew his brother. Cain might have been killed, and that would have put a termination to that line of human beings. This was not to

be, and the Lord put a mark upon him, which is the flat nose and black skin.

At this point you may be asking, "How could a just God curse the descendants of Cain for thousands of years over an event that happened at the dawn of humanity?" That's a good question, and Mormons were obviously thinking about it. One of the LDS Church's Articles of Faith reads: "We believe that men will be punished for their own sins, and not for Adam's transgression." This means that unlike most Christians, Mormons do not accept the idea of original sin, because it would be unfair for someone to go to hell because of a sin committed by someone else long ago. How then did the church justify denying black people the priesthood, and, by implication, entry into the celestial kingdom, based on Cain's crime? The Mormons developed an insidious answer to this question, and one that was used to justify not only withholding the priesthood from black people, but also the virulent opposition to the civil rights movement typified by Delbert Stapley and other members of the Mormon hierarchy.

In chapter 11, we introduced the Mormon belief that humans once lived in the presence of God as premortal spirits. In this premortal realm, our Heavenly Father solicited plans for how we might come to earth, obtain a physical body like his, and then return to live with him as perfected gods. Both Jesus and Lucifer presented plans to accomplish this, and when Jesus's plan was chosen, the followers of Lucifer rebelled, and a civil war broke out in heaven. The war ended when Lucifer and his minions were cast down from heaven and forever deprived of the opportunity to obtain a precious corporeal body. Those who sided with Jesus had earned the opportunity to come to earth. Nevertheless, some Mormon apostles and prophets have asserted that not everyone was particularly valiant in the war in heaven. While some fought hard for Jesus and his cause, others stood by idly waiting to see who would win. These "fence sitters" were not followers of

Lucifer, and so they were not cast out of heaven. But even though they were allowed to obtain bodies, they were destined to be born through a cursed lineage as punishment for their lack of commitment in the premortal existence. By now you've probably guessed that this cursed lineage was the seed of Cain. Hence, black people were cursed to go through life without the priesthood and marked as spiritually inferior because they were wishy-washy in a previous life. The influential Mormon theologian and prophet Joseph Fielding Smith made the case succinctly:

> There is a reason why one man is born black and with other disadvantages, while another is born white with great advantages. The reason is that we once had an estate before we came here, and were obedient, more or less, to the laws that were given us there. Those who were faithful in all things there received greater blessings here, and those who were not faithful received less. Every man had his agency there, and men receive rewards here based upon their actions there, just as they will receive rewards hereafter for deeds done in the body. The Negro, evidently, is receiving the reward he merits.

Fielding Smith's nephew, Bruce R. McKonkie, who succeeded his uncle as *de facto* church theologian and later became one of the twelve apostles, wrote:

> In the pre-existent eternity various degrees of valiance and devotion to the truth were exhibited by different groups of our Father's spirit offspring ... [S]ome were more valiant than others ... Those who were less valiant in pre-existence and who thereby had certain spiritual restrictions imposed upon them during mortality are known to us as the negroes. Such spirits are sent to earth through the lineage of Cain, the mark put upon him for his rebellion against God and his murder of Abel being a black skin ... Negroes in this life are denied the

priesthood; under no circumstances can they hold this delegation of authority from the Almighty ... It is the Lord's doing, is based on his eternal laws of justice, and grows out of the lack of spiritual valiance of those concerned in their first estate.

Mormon apologists acknowledge that this justification for the priesthood ban was widely taught, but they are quick to point out that it was never the official doctrine of the church. That may be true, but this belief was promulgated by Mormon leaders at the highest levels of power and authority, including prophets and apostles. Moreover, one of your authors (Phillips) is old enough to remember being taught this view without qualification or disclaimer both in seminary classes and in regular church meetings. It is safe to say that this justification for the priesthood ban was advanced as if it were doctrine and believed to be doctrine by most members of the church for the better part of a century.

Long after the civil rights movement, the church's ban on blacks receiving the priesthood remained in effect, and the idea that blacks were "fence sitters" in the premortal life remained the most common rationale for this discriminatory policy. But political pressure on the church began to mount. Sports teams from BYU faced protests over the church's race policy when they arrived on other campuses for events. The church's missionary efforts were severely hampered in Brazil, where interethnic marriage made it impossible to determine who was eligible for the priesthood and who was a descendant of Cain. Liberals from within the LDS church pointed to things like the ordination of Elijah Abel to call the legitimacy of the priesthood ban into question. Finally, in 1978, the policy was abruptly and completely disavowed, along with any justification used to support it.

The extent of this disavowal is illustrated by the case of BYU religion professor Randy Bott, who in February of 2012 was foolish enough to recount the story of the premortal "fence sitters" to a reporter for the *Washington Post*. The church was quick to denounce Bott for quoting the ideas set forth by Mormon proph-ets and apostles three decades ago. In a news release that was carried widely by major newspapers, a spokesman for the church wrote:

> The positions attributed to BYU professor Randy Bott in a recent *Washington Post* article absolutely do not represent the teachings and doctrines of The Church of Jesus Christ of Latter-day Saints. BYU faculty members do not speak for the Church. It is unfortunate that the Church was not given a chance to respond to what others said. The Church's position is clear – we believe all people are God's children and are equal in His eyes and in the Church. We do not tolerate racism in any form. For a time in the Church there was a restriction on the priesthood for male members of African descent. It is not known precisely why, how, or when this restriction began in the Church but what is clear is that it ended decades ago. Some have attempted to explain the reason for this restriction but these attempts should be viewed as speculation and opinion, not doctrine. The Church is not bound by speculation or opinions given with limited understanding. We condemn racism, including any and all past racism by individuals both inside and outside the Church.

We think this statement is striking. Condemnation of the words of a revered prophet like Joseph Fielding Smith is not a trivial matter. But the church has been working hard to live down its racist past, even if it has never offered an apology like the one put forth by the Southern Baptist Convention. The church has a robust missionary presence in Africa, and interracial marriages are now performed in Mormon temples. Nevertheless, racist ideas, including the idea of dark skin as a consequence of wickedness, persist in Mormon scripture.

Still, it is important to distinguish between a racist policy and its legacy, and racist attitudes and beliefs among members of the LDS church. Even before the priesthood ban was lifted in 1978, survey researchers noted that rank-and-file Mormons were more supportive of equality for blacks than the average American, and much more supportive than their conservative Christian counterparts. Hence, while the church policy was racist, the Mormon people, by and large, were not. This pattern persists to-day, and over 90 percent of Mormons say they would oppose a law banning interracial marriage, while over 98 percent claim they would vote for a black person for president (but not, appar-ently, Barack Obama). These sentiments make Mormons as pro-gressive as any major denomination on the issue of race.

So how does Mitt Romney fit into this picture? It is safe to assert that Mitt was taught in church that black people are suffering for their indolence in a premortal life. An apostle pretty much spelled out that view in a letter to Mitt's dad in 1964. But Mitt was probably also influenced by his parents, who were unshakable supporters of the civil rights movement and weren't at all swayed by the teachings of their church. Mitt has publicly stated that he was ecstatic when he heard that the church had reversed the priesthood ban – which is something that Mormons of Mitt's generation often say when they recall the events of 1978. We detect no hint of prejudice in Mitt Romney, just as we detect no hint of prejudice in the twenty-first-century Mormon church. Nevertheless, despite its public about-face, racist skeletons are moldering in the Mormon closet, and journalists seem to be prying the door open wider and wider. Whether or not the LDS church's regrettable history of racism becomes a major issue for candidate Mitt Romney remains to be seen.

suggestions for further reading

The definitive study on race issues in the Mormon church is Armand Mauss's *All Abraham's Children: Changing Mormon Conceptions of Race and Lineage* (University of Illinois Press, 2003). See also Newell G. Bringhurst and Darron T. Smith, *Black and Mormon* (University of Illinois Press, 2006). For a short treatise on the origin of the priesthood ban, see Stephen G. Taggart, *Mormonism's Negro Policy: Social and Historical Origins* (University of Utah Press, 1970). Jessie Embry's *Black Saints in a White Church: Contemporary African American Mormons* (Signature Books, 1994) presents oral histories of black Mormons and describes their experience with the church and its erstwhile policies. Another collection of oral histories is Cardell K. Jacobsen, *All God's Children: Racial and Ethnic Voices in the LDS Church* (Bonneville Books, 2004).

Part V: Looking Ahead

Would a Mormon president take orders from Salt Lake City?

CHAPTER EIGHTEEN

Would a Mormon president take orders from Salt Lake City?

the soundbite

Mormons stress obedience. It's a word you'll hear often in Mormon circles. They also repeat the mantra "follow the prophet" and believe that if you heed the words of the leaders in Salt Lake City, you won't be led astray. If Mitt Romney is a devout Mormon, then he probably believes this too. That's a very unsettling thought for people who worry that if he becomes president, Mitt will be beholden to the Mormon prophet and will take his marching orders from church headquarters in Salt Lake City. Is this a legitimate fear?

the details

Controversy over religious loyalties is nothing new to presidential elections. As the 1960 election drew near, people began to express concern over the candidacy of John F. Kennedy. Many feared that Kennedy, who was poised to become the nation's first Catholic president, would be a puppet for the Vatican and the United States would be ceding some of its sovereignty to the pope. In order to put these fears to rest, Kennedy delivered a now-famous speech outlining his views on the relationship between church and state. He stated:

> I believe in an America that is officially neither Catholic, Protestant nor Jewish; where no public official either

requests or accepts instructions on public policy from the pope, the National Council of Churches or any other ecclesiastical source; where no religious body seeks to impose its will directly or indirectly upon the general populace or the public acts of its officials.

Kennedy had to lay out it out plainly for the voting public: he would not let his religious loyalties affect his civic duties. The speech apparently allayed the fears of most Americans, because Kennedy won in a rout.

These days the same questions are being asked about Mitt Romney. Interestingly enough, we think the parallel between Kennedy and Romney has as much to do with the organizational structure of their respective churches as it does with matters of theology or religious devotion. Social scientists refer to the style of governance within a religious denomination as its "polity." Most major denominations in the United States are run by governing boards or councils, and an increasing number of churches are completely independent with no denominational affiliation whatsoever. In American Protestantism, it is rare to see an organization with substantial power vested in one person. But Catholicism and Mormonism are different. The pope stands at the head of the Catholic church, and according to canon law, he is infallible when speaking on matters of doctrine. The Mormon church is led by the prophet, who, like the pope, is appointed for life. Mormons do not believe that the prophet is infallible, but they do believe he is inspired. In conjunction with his counselors and the quorum of twelve apostles, the prophet can issue official edicts that are binding on the church. Such edicts are rare, but in 1995, the prophet Gordon B. Hinckley issued a proclamation declaring that "God has commanded that the sacred powers of procreation are to be employed only between man and woman, lawfully wedded as husband and wife." The unmistakable implication here is that God isn't keen on gay relationships. To believe otherwise is to be out of step with church doctrine.

Catholic leaders have been known to take action against politicians who have held positions contrary to church teaching. Representative Patrick Kennedy, the son of Senator Edward Kennedy, was barred from taking communion by his bishop because of his pro-choice politics. Could President Mitt Romney be similarly coerced into adopting policies that accord with Mormon teaching? After all, if the prophet is inspired, and if he can issue binding edicts, wouldn't a Mormon president be a marionette whose strings extended from Washington to Salt Lake City?

Before we give you our take on the matter, here's one thing to consider. In sacred ceremonies inside the temple, Mormons swear a solemn oath to obey "the law of God" and live in accordance with church teachings. This vow is called the Law of Obedience, and every Mormon who goes through the temple makes it. Moreover, the temple ceremony also asks Mormons to subscribe to the Law of Consecration – a promise to dedicate all one's time, talents, and material possessions to the church in order to prepare the way for the coming Kingdom of God. There is no doubt Mitt Romney made these vows, and vows made in the temple are a very serious matter for Mormons.

So could a Mormon elected official take a political stand that is contrary to church doctrine? Would a devout Mormon politician suffer consequences for defying the church? These are good questions, but they are unlikely to be relevant for Mitt Romney. While the church specifies matters of doctrine, it almost never dictates political positions. In the proclamation we quoted above, the church declares that sex outside of heterosexual marriage contravenes God's will, and the proclamation "call[s] upon re-sponsible citizens and officers of government everywhere to pro-mote those measures designed to maintain and strengthen the family as the fundamental unit of society."

Note, however, that they don't specify what those measures might be. God seems to be pretty specific about the kind of behavior he condones, but he's not too precise about how his edicts should be implemented in the public sphere.

A Mormon may believe, for instance, that abortion is a sin and still think we're better off if abortion is legal. That was Mitt Romney's position when he ran for the Senate in 1994. A Mormon may believe marriage is designed for a man and woman and still think it is unconstitutional to deny gay people the right to wed. This is precisely the position on gay marriage taken by Harry Reid, the senate majority leader and a devout Mormon. In a previous incarnation, Governor Mitt Romney was rather gay-friendly as well. He opposed an amendment to the Massachusetts constitution banning gay marriage and domestic partner benefits in the state, even though his wife and one of his sons were behind the initiative. There is no evidence that he was ever reprimanded by the church or that the church insisted he adopt a different position. Senator Reid's views are frequently at odds with the views of most Mormons, but he remains a member of the church in good standing, and there is not a scintilla of evidence that the church has ever told him what to do.

Once in a while the church will ask its members to mobilize for or against particular legislation. But this is not the same as a doctrinal decree. For instance, the church worked hard and contributed millions of dollars to defeat a gay marriage initiative in California. Nevertheless, many Mormons disagreed with the church's political activities, and some were even activists on the other side. We've never heard any credible reports that these dissenters were threatened with excommunication, although we bet things were awkward for them at Sunday meetings. Political purges may have happened in the past, but these days the LDS church does not punish people for their political views, so long as those views aren't wildly outside the mainstream.

One of the church's articles of faith states, "We believe in being subject to kings, presidents, rulers, and magistrates, in obeying, honoring, and sustaining the law." This statement undergirds the church's reluctance to get involved in politics and its complete avoidance of electoral politics. Despite the fact that Mitt Romney is the nation's most prominent Mormon, no member of the church's governing hierarchy has stepped forward to endorse his run for the White House. Church leaders simply don't do that sort of thing anymore. When they did in the past, it didn't work. In the 1930s and early 1940s, the church repeatedly published statements criticizing the social policies of Franklin Delano Roosevelt. But Roosevelt carried Utah in all four of his presidential bids.

This brings us to an important point about Mormons. Even when their leaders tell them exactly what to do, they don't always do it. The media likes to portray Mormons as brainwashed automatons, but the fact is that Mormons are gleefully engaged in all kinds of things their leaders think are sinful. The cities in Utah near our boyhood homes feature coffee shops, theaters playing rated-R movies, liquor stores, and tattoo parlors. All of these things are forbidden by the church, and yet some Mormons – who knows how many – engage in them without any fear of excommunication.

Mitt Romney avoids talking about Mormonism. It's not something he brings up on the stump, and the subject clearly makes him uncomfortable when it is broached in interviews. This might be because, as we've previously written, some people are uncomfortable with Mormon beliefs. But it is also the case that the church has said very little about Mitt Romney and his run for the White House. We think this reflects the church's desire to stay out of politics in general and electoral politics specifically. If Mitt wins, you can bet journalists will be looking for any evidence of a link between the White House and Salt Lake City. But aside from a few LDS advisors and confidants Mitt knows through ecclesiastical channels, they won't find one.

Besides, it is not necessary for the church to pull Mitt's strings. There is broad compatibility between the Republican Party platform and the church's positions on most issues. There won't be any need to tell him to do what he's inclined to do already. In sum, just as fears about JFK's ties to Catholicism turned out to be overblown, worries that Mitt Romney will be a mouthpiece for the Mormon prophet are greatly exaggerated.

suggestions for further reading

The majority of sources examining the LDS Church's involvement in politics deal with the complex relationship between the church and Utah's state government. Other sources look at the church's tumultuous relationship with the US government in the late nineteenth and early twentieth century. One of the few books focusing on the contemporary church and national politics is Lee Trepanier and Lynita K. Newsander, *LDS in the USA: Mormonism and the Making of American Culture* (Baylor University Press, 2012). A thorough study of Mormon political attitudes is Jeffrey C. Fox, *Latter-day Political Views* (Lexington Books, 2006).

CONCLUSION

Mitt Romney is not the first Mormon to run for president. Joseph Smith, the very first Mormon, launched a presidential campaign. Mitt's father George did as well. Mormons are a civic-minded people, and they tend to be overrepresented relative to their numbers at all levels of government. But the 2012 election is unprecedented, because it is the first time a member of the LDS church has a realistic shot at winning the White House. This has put Mormonism under a brighter spotlight than ever before. And if polling data are correct, people don't like what they see. Americans are more hostile to Mormons than any other major religious tradition besides Muslims. This is an acknowledged headache for the church, and it is potentially dangerous for the Romney candidacy. But is it justified? In this book we've attempted to demystify Mormonism and strip away fact from fantasy. Even so, some of you may still be thinking the unvarnished truth about Mormon practice and theology is just too weird, and voting for someone who believes such weirdness is too risky. After all, that's what students tell us, and if polls are accurate, that's what lots of Americans think.

If you're still opposed to the idea of a Mormon president for religious reasons, let us take one last stab at convincing you that what makes Mormonism weird in the eyes of the public is the fact that it is unfamiliar, and the unfamiliar always seems strange. Mormonism is like an exotic cuisine you've only seen in pictures. You'd never put that in your mouth. But someone raised on that cuisine might find those pictures appetizing and think what *you* eat is disgusting. Our point here is that any Christian denomina-tion would seem bizarre to you if it was as unfamiliar and as unfairly maligned by the media as Mormonism. To prove it, let's compare the peculiar characteristics of the Mormon church to some of the nation's most upstanding, high-profile, respectable denominations.

Let's start with polygamy. Nothing about Mormonism provokes more outrage than polygamy. Even modern-day Mormons are pretty grossed out by it. You may think no reasonable person would ever affiliate with a religious movement founded by a notorious, profligate womanizer and anyone with ancestors who engaged in such a sexist, licentious practice should repudiate it without equivocation. But would you expect the same thing of Episcopalians? The Episcopal church is one of the nation's most respected religious bodies. More US presidents have been members of the Episcopal church than any other denomination. Yet this church traces its roots to the sexual escapades of its first leader. The Episcopal church in the United States is a member of the Anglican Communion, and thus an arm of the Church of England. The Church of England was founded when the pope refused to annul the marriage of King Henry VIII and Catharine of Aragon. Henry wanted a much younger woman, and rather than submit to the pope and stay with his wife, he initiated a schism with Rome and was installed as head of a new church. Thus, the Episcopal church owes its existence to a horny ruler who wanted to commit what was then seen as adultery with impunity.

What about the temple? Shouldn't a man who engages in secret rites with strange ritual vestments be disqualified from the highest office in the land? Well, recall that a number of US presidents have been Freemasons and that the masonic rituals formed the basis of Mormon temple worship. Would you be concerned about voting for a Freemason? Moreover, Catholics come together on Sunday, chant their creeds in unison, and consume representations of the flesh and blood of their god administered by a man in a gown. This grossly unfair description of the Mass is not far off from the unfair descriptions we've seen of Mormon temple worship. It's true that only the officiators wear funny clothes in Catholic churches and that Catholics don't much care who observes the Mass, but aside from these distinctions, if you'd never heard of Catholics before, it would be easy to lump their weird rituals in with the weirdness that goes on in Mormon temples.

But what could be stranger than Kolob? How could we trust a man with the nuclear launch codes if he believes he knows the name of the star God's home planet orbits? We admit that Kolob is a head-scratcher. Nevertheless, based on a dubious interpretation of a single Bible verse (First Thessalonians 4:17), millions of Evangelical Christians, including a few who were early contenders for the Republican nomination, believe they will one day defy gravity and fly up into the sky to meet Jesus when he returns, leaving all the non-Christians to fend for themselves in a world consumed by evil. They call this event the rapture. There are obvious logistical problems associated with the rapture: Will Christians in Kansas and Christians in China rendezvous in one spot, or will Jesus make an appearance in each time zone? But attacking this belief because it mocks the laws of physics completely misses the point. All religions have beliefs that mock the laws of physics. If you're going to disqualify Mormons because they believe things that are far-fetched, you'll need to disqualify almost every devoutly religious person eligible to be president, regardless of his or her faith. It's just easier for most people to single out Mormonism because they've never heard of Kolob. But since a man living three days in a fish's belly, floods that cover the whole earth, and Machiavellian talking snakes are part of their cultural heritage, they give folks who believe these things a pass. There is as much empirical evidence for the existence of Kolob as there is for any of Jesus's miracles: none. We could go on forever, but by now you get the point. Theological weirdness is in the eye of the beholder, and most religious people believe some things with no scientific basis.

What if theology isn't your concern? What if you're a progressive and you disagree with the Mormon church's views on homosexuality and women's rights? We're concerned about these things too, and it's partly why neither of us is voting for Mitt Romney. But these issues are not just Mormon issues. They are *Republican* issues. It's simply impossible to tell which aspects of Mitt Romney's stand on social issues stem from his Mormonism and which come from his political proclivities. Frankly, we don't think the distinction matters, and it is worth noting that no candidate with moderate views on social issues could have won the Republican nomination this year.

We hope you will select a candidate this election who sees eye to eye with you on the issues. That's what we're going to do. We don't think Mitt Romney's Mormonism disqualifies him for the Presidency or constitutes a sound reason why you or anyone else should vote against him. Could you vote for a Mormon for president? We could. But this time, we won't.

ABOUT THE AUTHORS

Ryan T. Cragun is an Assistant Professor of Sociology at the University of Tampa. His research interests include Mormonism and the nonreligious. He is the author of more than a dozen peer-reviewed articles and half a dozen book chapters. His research has been published in such journals as: *Sociology of Religion, Dialogue: A Journal of Mormon Thought, Journal for the Scientific Study of Religion, Journal of Contemporary Religion, Journal of Religion and Health, Mental Health, Religion and Culture,* and *Nova Religio*. His research has been featured in numerous local and national newspapers, including: *Tampa Bay Times, the Salt Lake Tribune, the Washington Post, the Huffington Post,* and *Bloomberg Business Week*. Dr. Cragun is also a past president of the Mormon Social Science Association.

Rick Phillips is an Associate Professor of Sociology at the University of North Florida. He is the author of one book and more than a dozen articles on Mormonism. His research has been published in such journals as: *Sociology of Religion, Journal for the Scientific Study of Religion,* and *Nova Religio*. Dr. Phillips is a former president of the Mormon Social Science Association, a scholarly association of social scientists interested in the study of Mormonism.

www.ingramcontent.com/pod-product-compliance
Lightning Source LLC
Chambersburg PA
CBHW051805040426
42446CB00007B/532